Resume Strategies in the Age of COVID-19 and the Post-Pandemic Era

AL PALUMBO, CPRW, MBA

Certified Professional Resume Writer

Contents

Chapter 1   7
How COVID has Changed the Hiring Landscape

Chapter 2   9
Addressing the Covid-19 Layoff on Resumes,
Cover Letters, and LinkedIn Profiles

Chapter 3   13
The Building Components of a Resume

Chapter 4   21
Resume Myths

Chapter 5   23
Organizing Your Job Search

Chapter 6   27
The Resume Building Process

Chapter 6   43
Job Winning Resumes that Work

Appendix   109

> **Is your resume a job description or a marketing tool that demonstrates your value?**

> **Advice about applicant tracking system software that companies use to select applicants for interviews.**

> **Are you a Do-er or an Achiever? What does your resume say you are?**

> **When it comes to resumes, don't put the cart before the horse. Target the job before you write!**

> **The art of the cover letter.**

INTRODUCTION

As a Professional Resume Writer, I can attest that the demand for resume writing, cover letter, and LinkedIn profile services has skyrocketed. Some folks are out of work because COVID-19 has impacted their careers. My clients often do not know where to begin, but they realize that their resumes need a makeover. In today's job market, it is not enough to write a pretty resume. You need to create resumes that employers will see. Today, opportunities can be in the office or remote because of social distancing. Many employees and employers are finding out that working remotely has its advantages, and I think COVID-19 has helped launch a work at home trend for the professional workforce.

As I write this, Americans are being vaccinated. Over the past year, many employers suspended hiring activities because of the uncertainty about the virus's long-term impact. The good news is that employers are starting to hire again, which will increase as their confidence in the economy and America's recovery increases. Now is the best time to prepare for a fast re-entry into the job market. It is a good time for reflection and a good time to research employers, perfect resumes and social media platforms, and expand your network with professionals inside and outside your industry. You can bet that industries will be experiencing increased demand for goods and services, and particular job growth will include businesses such as health care, pharmaceuticals, grocery chains, delivery services, and online purchasing.

As a result of the Pandemic, more people have begun to work remotely and new opportunities for working remotely are already here. New businesses and services are emerging for graduating students and the seasoned workforce alike. This is a great time to research employers that you may want to work for, understand their requirements, perhaps take some courses online to increase skills and make you more employable.

Did you ever file for a job online, and you KNEW that you were eminently qualified but never heard back from the employer? Despite your qualifications, your resume went into *the Black Hole of Cyber-Space*! In my job-seeking adventures and working with thousands of clients, I have learned how to make a resume stand out in the crowd. You cannot simply write a resume or have it written for you and think you are finished.

To be competitive, you need to "tweak" your resume or maybe have several versions of it, depending on your career goals. I recently had a client who had a degree in Public Administration but worked in retail her entire career. She now wanted to make a career change. The resume that I produced for her cast her in a whole new light, without exaggerating or being overly "creative." I took full advantage of her "transferable" skills in retail that related to her new target. I also focused on her studies. After all, the curriculum she followed was packed with keywords and skills that employers in the public sector were looking for.

The new resume had to demonstrate her ability to work in the public sector. I produced her "makeover," and it has worked for her. However, if she decided she wanted to go back to retail, the resume I wrote wouldn't work too well. If she wanted flexibility in applying to a range of jobs, I recommended that she need two resumes. Much of the information would be similar, but the original resume's focus and keywords would need to change.

To have the best chance in the post-COVID era, you should update your resume to align your background, education, and experience with the positions you are looking for today.

I used to spend a lot of time agonizing over formats for my resume. I have ended the agony by identifying formats that have worked for me and subsequently for my clients. Examples of resumes across a range of occupations are provided in the last chapter.

Here is what I recommend: Make your resume easy to read. We call this providing "white space." I will explain what the best resume practices are in the 2020s. For example, did you know that your resume doesn't have to be only one page? Don't make the reader have to guess if you are a good fit. Make it evident from the first line in your resume. Show that your skill set aligns with what they are looking for in a candidate, know your value, and show it!

1

How COVID-19 Has Changed the Hiring Landscape

What a challenging time to be job searching! By April 2021, there were 22 million Americans who lost their jobs because of the impact of the Pandemic. Job prospects indeed seem daunting as we endure the highest rate of unemployment since the Great Depression.

COVID forced many businesses to put hiring on hold, but other industries never stopped hiring. Most available jobs were in government, government contracting, transportation, delivery, healthcare, cybersecurity, and tech start-ups. Many tech and software professionals were not affected by COVID-19 and were already working remotely before the Pandemic shut everything down.

Despite the COVID debacle, this is an excellent time to launch or continue your job search. Let's contemplate how to adjust the approach to job hunting. Recruiters report that a prospective candidate who is desperate to become employed often mistakes quantity for quality when applying for work. Suppose you are creating a general resume and plastering it across the internet at every job opportunity. In that case, your resumes will likely be weeded out by software that HR departments in all the Fortune 500 companies are using, known as "Applicant Tracking Systems" or ATS.

There is a better way to go about this. I often recommend creating a master resume listing all skills, certifications, education, and work experience. The next step is to tweak the resume each time you are responding to a job posting. The posting will almost always tell you what the company wants in a candidate. Specific **keywords** are used to describe qualifications, skills, and experience. Tailor the resume into a one or two-page document and keep the things that the employer is seeking.

Finding job vacancies takes a bit of research. You can go on job boards like Indeed.com, enter a job title that you are interested in applying for, and a list of job postings will appear. But it would be best if you also considered researching all the companies you would consider working for or that you know are looking to hire. Companies do not always advertise but look for employees through word-of-mouth, recommendations, social media platforms or post open jobs in a careers link on their websites.

the post-COVID-19 era, it is time to be flexible and not rigid about your career. The Pandemic will not last forever, but right now, there may not be jobs in your field, and this may be an opportunity to expand your experience and your employability. Focus on what your skills are and think about how "transferable" they are to other occupations.

It is always tougher to look for employment when you don't have a job, and job seekers worry about how potential employers will view the gap in employment on your resume. Of course, this doesn't make much sense given the hell this country has gone through. It is irrational. Millions of excellent workers are out of work due to this unprecedented time, and I believe employers are not as likely to be worried about unemployed job seekers right now. During the Great Recession of 2008, most employers understood that people were laid off due to circumstances beyond their control.

One of the best ways to address an employment gap on your resume is to demonstrate that you have used this time to volunteer, learn a new skill, or take on new paid or unpaid responsibilities. Most modern resumes rely on a chronologically formatted resume, listing experience in reverse, starting with the most recent position. Recruiters are generally skeptical of other types of resume formats, such as the Functional Resume, especially when employment dates are omitted or obscured.

As with any layoff, you don't want to focus your resume and cover letter on the fact that you were let go. You can clarify that you were laid off because of COVID-19, but don't go into excessive detail. It would suffice to add to the last position, "role was eliminated due to company downsizing after COVID". Your cover letter can provide some additional detail but shouldn't focus on the termination.

2

Addressing the COVID-19 Layoff on Resumes, Cover Letters, and LinkedIn Profiles

WHAT ARE EMPLOYERS LOOKING FOR IN THE POST-COVID ERA?

By April 2021, close to 100 million Americans have been vaccinated. In the COVID-19 era, job searching hasn't ended, but it has changed. Just as hiring occurred in past recessions and the market crash of 2008, hiring still happens and it is happening now. However, we are experiencing a "new normal" in the hiring process. For companies to emerge stronger from the Pandemic, they need to hire candidates with the right skills.

They are focusing on candidates who can:

- Create new streams of revenue by hiring candidates who have proven their value to the organizations they have worked for. Your resume needs to show that you can deliver for the company by including measurable accomplishments.

- Many companies realize that they can cut costs with remote workers. You can provide an edge to other candidates if you can show how you have streamlined operations, saved costs, or increased production. This portrays you as someone who can help companies emerge from this crisis.

- If you are a project manager, the ability to hire, train, and manage remote teams, especially during the Pandemic, should be highlighted. In many ways, we are already in a virtual work climate.

- In tandem with the virtual work climate is the ability to overcome challenges despite uncertainty or ambiguity. Your resume should highlight instances where you solved problems without precedents,

Most people don't think to update their resume or LinkedIn profile until they are ready to start their "formal" job search or are forced into job searching. Now is a good time to focus on updating your resume and LinkedIn profile. If a recruiter asks for your resume today, are you ready to send one? Is it optimized for the job search?

VACCINATE YOUR RESUME!

Vaccinate your resume against ATS systems by adding key words and accomplishments!

If you were laid off during this Pandemic, you probably have an employment gap on your resume. If this is the case, don't sweat it because a lot of job applicants are in the same boat. Don't hide the gaps in your resume. Put in a statement after your most current job that you were laid off due to the COVID-19 Pandemic.

We can go further than that if you have been engaged in any meaningful activities during your time off from work. Perhaps this includes self-development, such as taking training courses and obtaining certifications. Hopefully, these skill sets can add to the "keywords" your resume should have.

Perhaps you became involved in caregiving for vulnerable people or was involved in community or voluntary work efforts. In this case, you can help fill the gap by describing this as the most recent entry in your resume. Remember, experience is experience, whether paid or voluntary.

Don't neglect technical and digital skills on your resume. Companies are transitioning into remote work situations, and highlighting your skills provides you with an advantage. This includes communication tools such as Zoom and other technologies. If you have worked remotely, add this as a keyword.

Soft skills are also important. You want to describe yourself as adaptable and open to change, using words like adaptability, self-motivation, and change management.

THERE ARE NO JOBS IN MY CURRENT FIELD BECAUSE OF COVID-19

Some occupations have been slammed by Covid, including jobs related to hospitality and tourism, and this may be a time for a career change. If this is the case, the focus should be on transferable skills that relate to the new occupational area.

If you have had to accept a short-term job during the Pandemic, employers will likely understand that you accepted these positions to stay employed during the Pandemic.

Applicants often get discouraged during economic downturns. With an updated resume that is written to the jobs you are seeking, as addressed throughout this book, you are more equipped than you may think you are.

THE COVER LETTER

While the resume summarizes your background, accomplishments, and skills, it is fairly straightforward and leaves little room to expand or explain. Here is where the cover letter can be a big assist in your job search.

Your cover letter can address employment gaps and other issues by using the cover letter to connect our skills to the employer's needs. A hiring manager not only wants to know that you have the skills for the job, but they need to assess if you would be a good fit for their team. You can use the cover letter to expand on how you have made a team successful. Let them see how you can provide the same collaborative spirit for their team.

The cover letter, like your resume, and LinkedIn profile, are marketing tools for your brand. It is your sales pitch. Let your cover letter clearly state your value. The job poster has probably described the profile of the candidate they are seeking. Mirror this with your own story. Make it fit their profile. Make the recruiter's job easier. Spell out why they need you.

THE LINKEDIN PROFILE (AKA SOCIAL MEDIA BIO)

Although the focus of this book is the Resume, the fastest way to a new job is through networking, and a great tool for networking is the LinkedIn Profile. In the time of COVID-19, decision-makers are more accessible and open to communication, just because of the social isolation that the Pandemic caused. The global marketplace is as competitive as ever and improving or establishing an online presence will help you in your networking efforts.

The first item noticed by others will be your Professional Headline. This pops up in a LinkedIn search. LinkedIn provides you with 220 characters in this section that you can use to garner attention. Creativity in the Headline will help you stand out. LinkedIn uses keywords to determine how your profile ranks in search results of employers. Elsewhere I describe how to identify keywords for your resume. Put them in your LinkedIn Profile.

I am contacted regularly by employers seeking certified resume writers, and I am not soliciting them, they are soliciting me. I think it is wise to ad a Branding Statement under the Headline. "Stronger than Dirt" worked well for a laundry detergent. What should your branding statement be? It all depends on what you are selling.

Examples:
Career Coach: " Helping clients reassess their life choices to discover their true paths to success."
Marketer: " Developing sustainable business models and marketing strategies to drive small business growth.

LinkedIn allows you to have a background banner on your profile, such as a photograph or logo. If you decide to add something, remember that this is a professional networking tool, so don't include beach photos. Try to select something that resonates with your brand.

Next comes the **"About"** section. The first 270 characters are visible without the viewer having to select the "see more" button. The total number of characters are 2,600, so this section should clearly state your value proposition. When you write your profile, talk in the first person. Personal pronouns are ok on the LinkedIn profile, but not your resume.

"Skills Endorsements and Recommendations" is the skills section. Hard skills and soft skills belong here, and the first three entries should contain the top keywords that relate to your career goals. Try to get colleagues to endorse your skills and provide recommendations.

Don't forget that you can customize your URL. Log in and click on the "me" icon on your LinkedIn homepage. Click View Profile, Click Edit Public Profile & URL on the right side of your screen. Click Edit public profile & URL on the right side of your screen. Under Edit your custom URL, click the ✎ Edit icon next to your public profile URL. Put the LinkedIn URL on your resume in the contact section of the resume.

3

The Building Components of a Resume

To write the most effective resume, you need to start with the premise that your resume is a marketing tool that, if skillfully written, presents the reader with a picture of your knowledge, skills, abilities, work history, and the value that you have brought to the organization throughout your career.

I can remember when you didn't necessarily need a resume to get hired. If you were well known in your industry, job changes usually came out of your network. You probably had to submit a resume, but you were already on the radar screen, so the resume you used then probably wouldn't work now.

During the Pandemic, and in the post-Covid 19 era, resumes are and will be used to screen applicants for interviews based on an assessment that you will most closely match the employer's needs. Fortune 500 companies and many of today's larger employers are screening resumes to *eliminate* those that do not appear to be a good match. They have invested in "Applicant Tracking Systems," or ATS.

Resume Formats

The three most common resume formats are Chronological, Functional, and Hybrid.

The **Chronological Format** is generally preferred by hiring managers because it can demonstrate continuous career growth, working in reverse chronology from the most recent or current job first. This will allow you to expand on your job functions and accomplishments for each position listed.

The **Functional Resume** emphasizes skills, abilities, education, and other credentials and accomplishments at the beginning of the resume but does not align with any specific previous employer. I prefer not o use the Functional Resume format because recruiters don't like them. Many hiring managers consider this to be the format of choice for job hoppers, employment gaps, and applicants with limited experience. The assumption is that the applicant has a reason not to list employment history chronologically and invites more scrutiny, assuming it is even read.

The **Hybrid Format** is my favorite format, and this is the format to focus on for the rest of this book. This format highlights skills and accomplishments, doesn't hide work history gaps, is front-loaded to provide hiring managers with the most relevant information first, and appeals to traditional and non-traditional employers.

Please keep in mind that hiring managers will not necessarily read the entire resume at first glance. As a hiring manager, I looked for position titles, employment dates, skillsets of the applicant, and how they matched with the applicant I was looking for.

The Hybrid Format:

Resume Sections

Section	
Heading →	**John Jameson** Tampa, FL 33609 • 813-555-1234 • jjameson@gmail.com • www.linkedin.com/in/jamiej/
Headline →	**Sales Representative**
Profile →	Self-motivated, confident sales professional with proven ability to develop customer relationships that provide a competitive edge in a challenging environment. Identify the needs of customers and demonstrate how products and services that enable growth. Work independently and collaboratively to meet and exceed sales targets through tenacity and ability to close.
Core Skills (keywords) →	**Core Skills** Client Relationship Building | Sales Presentations | Lead Generation | Prospecting | Consultative Sales Techniques Product Knowledge | Product Solutions | Marketing Intelligence | Competitive Analysis | Account Management Post-Sales Servicing | Client Retention | Client Pipeline Management | Sales Cycle Management
Job History →	**Professional Experience** **ACME WIDGET SOLUTIONS – Lexington, MA | 2019 – 2021** • Sold full product line to warm prospects from leads furnished and from prospecting. • Applied knowledge of products and client needs to present solutions to help clients grow their business. • Attained the highest sales revenue among a ten-member sales team, representing a 50% increase in assigned territory sales. • Expanded business into new markets by studying the competition and identifying and cultivating decision-makers, leading to a 20% increase in company growth in 2020. **MAVERICK CONSTRUCTION SERVICES – Peoria, AZ | 2015 – 2019** • Turned-around, a construction company that had four years of decreasing sales by developing key relationships with realtors, architects, and public agencies. • Built revenue from $1 million annually to $7 million by entering into strategic business partnerships and providing niche services not offered universally within the market.
Education →	**Education** **B.S. Business Administration –** Phoenix University
Professional Development →	**Professional Development** Sales Techniques Certificate – Red Canyon Community College CRM Applications and Usage in the Sales Process – Maxwell Technical Institute
Technology →	**Technology Summary** MS Word, MS Excel, MS PowerPoint, MS Outlook, Salesforce.com. CRM

The Executive or Career Summary

Perhaps the most important section of your resume is the Executive or Career Summary. This is a short statement, no more than five compelling sentences that emphasize your relevant strengths and experiences. Here, you provide the employer with a value proposition: hire me because this is what I can deliver to the organization. It basically should answer the employer's question, "Why should we hire you"?

Professional resume writers refer to this section as "the elevator pitch." It is what makes you stand out in the crowd by showcasing strengths and transferable skills. It is effective only if it targets a specific job aligned with the needs of employers. As a hiring manager, I can read the first few lines in this resume that will let me know if your resume merits further review. Like I said before, it only takes about six seconds for an employer to decide if your resume is worth the time to read it. When you write this way, you control the story and the brand you are presenting.

THE HEADING:

This is where your contact information is provided. With so many people working from home during the COVID-19 process, it became less important to list your resume's actual residence. While you still can, it is no longer necessary. Odds are you will be contacted by phone or email if your resume is selected for follow-up, and not snail mail. It's your choice. It's not wrong to list your full address, but you don't have to. It's your choice.

Some words of caution: if you are still working, don't list your contact information at your employer's location (phone, company email). Why? It is unprofessional and can give the false impression that you spend your time on the job hunting for your next one. Also, get rid of emails your friends may think are cute and use a professional one. I recommend some form of your name, such as johnjames@yahoo.com. Just make sure you check It dally during u live career search.

THE HEADLINE:

The resume headline should focus the employer on your candidacy for the job that has been advertised. If they are looking for a Territory Sales Manager and you have credentials for this position, I suggest you title your Headline as "Territory Sales Manager." Your job title may not exactly match this, but if this is what you are qualified to do, it is a better choice than "Career Summary" or "Career Profile" or another non-descript title.

HIGHLIGHTS – CORE SKILLS:

This section of the resume allows you to put keywords representing your soft and hard skills right upfront. Ideally, they should align with keywords that the employer has used in the job posting. If they are using ATS, they will scan and track your resume and match it to the algorithms in their program to identify a match of keywords. This results in a higher score and separates your resume from that of other applicants who didn't take care to revise their resume for the job they are applying for. I will demonstrate this in a later chapter and show you how you can make the employer's posting work for you.

Soft skills are skills that you have acquired during your life as a student and in the workplace. You will often see soft skills described in typical job postings. These are often referred to as "people skills." If they post it, I recommend you find a way to place these in your resume. Here are some examples of soft skills:

Active Listening, Communication, Interpersonal Skills, Team Leadership, Problem-solving, Detail Oriented, Time Management, Relationship Building, Training, Mentoring, Empathy, Adaptability, Willingness to Learn

Hard Skills are mostly job-specific skills, often of a technical or professional nature. Hard skills are often teachable, so if you studied a particular subject in school, your resume should claim the hard skills learned in the classroom or internships. If you have been in the workforce, you have hard skills extremely valuable to the employer. Consider the following statement, which contains hard and soft skills within the sentence. *"**Detail-oriented** software developer skilled in **Python, C, C++,** and **other computer programming languages**."* Whether this phrase is included in the Executive Summary at the top of your resume, or in the Highlights section, if the employer listed these skills, an ATS will find it in a resume scan, or an employer will eyeball it in reviewing your resume personally.

Every job requires certain **technical/hard skills** specific to that industry. Here are some examples:

Bilingual French/English, Database Management, Microsoft Office Suite, SEO/SEM Marketing, Statistical Analysis, Project Management, Market Campaign Management, Programming Languages, Continuous Process Improvement, Lean Manufacturing, Risk Mitigation

Bullet points are a great way to generate lists that are easy to read, enabling a quick way to present your skills in less space, while providing critical information. You don't need to exaggerate or embellish your background. You should be able to defend or demonstrate your skills during an interview. You need to be conversant about any skills you list in the resume.

Keywords and the Applicant Tracking System (ATS)

ATS is an applicant tracking system software that facilitates recruiting and hiring functions. These systems can collect and sort thousands of resumes. Much hiring comes from applicants who have applied for jobs online, either through an employer's website or a job board (e.g., Indeed.com). The resume is not going directly to HR. First, it is processed by an ATS. Who knows if a human recruiter will ever look at it? It all depends on how your resume stands up to ATS algorithms. Most successful employers hire for multiple jobs at once and can receive hundreds of resumes in response to a single job posting. In times past, the hiring manager would have to sift through this pile to put together a short-stack of applicants. From my personal experience as a hiring manager, I can tell you that it took no more than *six seconds* to decide if I was going to read the whole thing.

Today, applying for a job online is pretty simple, temping applicants who are unqualified to give it a shot. The ATS enables the identification of top candidates, essentially helping the hiring manager to lower the pool of applicants. Applicant tracking systems collect and store resumes in a database for access by hiring professionals. Even after a job is filled, resumes can be stored for a long time and are searched and sorted. Applicant tracking systems compare your resume to the job posting. Some recruiters will opt to glance at all resumes that come in but will likely invest about six seconds on each before moving on to the next one.

Hopefully, the employer's ATS will score your resume higher than others, warranting further review. Candidates who can review a job posting and predict the correct resume keywords will have the greatest chance of being included in candidate search results.

Employers utilize many different ATS. Here are some of them: Taleo, Workday Success, Factors, Greenhouse, BrassRing, iCIMS, Jobvite, Lever, SmartRecruiters, JazzHR, CATS, and Bamboo HR.

Every time you post your resume online, recruiters and hiring managers can find you based on the keywords you have placed in your resume. Employers scan resumes for these keywords, and their systems filter them and rank them. If your resume doesn't have the right search words or is formatted in a not ATS-friendly way, the resume can be dispatched to the black hole of cyberspace.

To some degree, Applicant Tracking Systems are not fail-safe. Some qualified candidates can be automatically filtered out by mistake during resume vetting, and this calls for some additional strategizing. The best systems have overcome many of the drawbacks of earlier systems in use. Leave nothing to chance, because there are ways to optimize your resume to stand up to the ATS. Make your resume ATS friendly. Here is how:

- Use the right font, ensuring that the ATS can "read" your content. Some systems stumble over Times New Roman font, one of the most popular. These systems have trouble reading Serif font because of the slight marks that are within their letters. Avoid Times New Roman, Cambria, and other similar fonts.

I recommend Sans Serif fonts. I prefer Calibri and Calibri Light, and their cousin Arial.

- The best bullet points for ATS are ocular or round shape fonts. Avoid using arrows and other symbols. They may look good to the eye but can wreak havoc on Applicant Tracking Systems, jumbling your text in the scanning process.
- Avoid PDF, HTML, Open Office, and Apple Pages formats. While certain Applicant Tracking Systems can handle some of these formats, most cannot, especially older systems. Stick with a Word document file.
- Don't put important information in a header or footer on your Word document. The ATS will not be able to scan that content.
- Don't use photographs, text boxes, graphics, or tables. These will inhibit the proper scanning of your resume.
- Format your resume by tabbing it for columns, such as in the Highlights example shown in the resume sample illustrated above.

PROFESSIONAL EXPERIENCE

This is the employment section of your resume and has an important impact on a prospective employer's determination to grant an applicant interview. This section emphasizes experience and accomplishments. Working backward from your current or last position, this section should not simply be a condensed job description.

While the resume should provide a good idea of your job functions, the focus should be on specific accomplishments and achievements that made the organization better because of your contributions. Your accomplishments on the resume are far more impactful than a description of day-to-day functions. I cannot begin to tell you how gut-wrenching it is to read a resume that describes every single detail about what you do on the job. There is no earthly reason to put such a level of detail into the resume. When your resume is accomplishment-driven, it screams to the employer the value that you could bring to their organization.

Accomplishments can be qualitative or quantitative. Here are examples:

Quantitative Accomplishments: Numeric data that show increases in profit or revenue, the dollar value of cost savings to the company, reduction in the cost of inventory, increased in specific key performance indicators that measure success such as customer retention rates and prospect conversion rates.

Qualitative Accomplishments: Often, clients will tell me that they don't have the numbers to show accomplishments. That's when we pivot to Qualitative accomplishments. You can consider some of the following: Awards and recognition, the introduction of new technology that resulted in process improvements, mergers and acquisitions, problem resolution and its impact on the organization, new policy and procedures and their impact on the organization, systems enhancements, quality improvements, and so on.

THE EDUCATION SECTION

If you have a college degree or degrees, list the highest-level degree first and then work back: Ph.D., Masters, Bachelors, Associate. There is no hard and fast rule about where to place this section of your resume.

Generally, if I am writing for a recent graduate, I want to put it right after the Highlights Section and before Employment. As your career progresses, you should provide more focus on experience and accomplishments, and the resume can descend toward the bottom. There is no rule regarding the placement of the Education Section. If I am writing a resume for a Technology professional and the degree is super-relevant, I will usually place this section before Employment, especially if it is critical to the position.

OTHER SECTIONS

Military Experience with an honorable discharge can be listed on your resume. If the military experience is directly related to the civilian position, your experience can be listed as part of your work history or in a separate section entitled "Military". No rules are governing this. For example, if you worked on F-35s as an Air Force mechanic and want to do similar work as a civilian, the transition would flow nicely if placed in the WORK EXPERIENCE section of the resume.

Interests and Hobbies can add additional information that is interesting to employers, especially if these relate to your career goals. I generally do not include this on a resume unless it is provocative and adds to your qualifications and experience. Other resume writers may disagree, but it is a matter of your preference. I prefer not to list anything that doesn't add to the "sell".

Professional Affiliations and Memberships should be included in your resume. If you have provided community service by volunteering, it can portray you as invested in the community and provide service to the community. It speaks to your commitment and character. If you sit on a Board of Directors, it demonstrates that you are respected in the industry and add distinction. Memberships and trade associations, when listed, show that you are a contributing member of your profession.

Technical and Computer Skills are an important part of your resume, and I will provide examples of how to show this in the last chapter. Especially if you are an IT Professional, you will find that job postings call out technical skills such as specific software applications and programming experience. If the job posting calls these out and you have these skills, they should be listed. I prefer to show this in a separate section on the resume. If you are a non-IT manager, I frequently will put this on the first page of your resume under the Highlights Section. Again, there are no rules regarding placement, but if this is an important requirement, it shouldn't get lost at the bottom of your resume.

Licenses and Certifications should be listed on your resume if they are relevant to the job you are applying for. I recommend that this be put into its section on the resume.

Language skills are often an important factor in the Post-COVIC-19 multicultural world that we live in. If these skills are critical, they should be placed in the Highlights section of your resume. Otherwise, they can be noted near the end.

Personal Information is best omitted in a resume intended for the U.S. market. Date of birth, marital status, health, number of dependents, etc., can be used to discriminate based on age, race, religion, and other factors. For this reason, most personal information should be eliminated. If personal information does not improve your chances to get an interview, there is no reason to include it.

4

Resume Myths

Myth No. 1: My resume Has to be one page.

Unless an employer has specifically requested a one-page resume, the length of your resume should be based on your experience, your accomplishments, and other information that makes you an appealing candidate. I often have to debate with clients about expanding their resumes. Consider this: There is no "one-page resume" rule. Two or even three pages may be appropriate. I tell clients that a skilled HR recruiter can know within six seconds whether your resume is worth the time to read it. That is why all the important stuff needs to be on page one. Also, consider that his boss has tasked an HR recruiter to provide a handful of qualified applicants.

There is a certain amount of due diligence that comes with selecting qualified candidates.   Recent graduates usually can start their career search with a one-page resume. However, there are instances where academic and other activities provide information that is critical to getting the interview, and I advise college students to go to a two-page maximum only if we can't fit all of their experience, accomplishments, and credentials on one page.

Myth No. 2: The COVID employment gap on my resume will hurt my chances for work.

The downturn in the economy caused by COVID left many people out of work and now have gaps in their work history. You may want to include a line on the resume or cover letter to explain this.

Myth No. 3: A Good Resume gets the Job.

A good resume gets the interview. Good performance during the interview gets the job. The resume should be a blueprint of accomplishments and demonstrate the value you can bring to the new employer based on past accomplishments. The interview grants the opportunity to expand on these points.

Myth 4: Using the Same Resume Over and Over

You can send out 50 resumes in one day and accomplish absolutely nothing. If you use the same resume for different job opportunities and do not take the time to customized it, you may be disappointed in the results. I advocate customizing your resume for each job that you apply for. Recruiters get excited when they see a diamond in the rough, especially after sorting through 50 or 60 resumes from unqualified candidates.

Myth 5: Resumes should include your entire work history.

I often tell my clients that a resume is not a biography and not a detailed job description. After all, recruiters have short attention spans and do not want to read multiple pages of irrelevant detail. If a job is not relevant, remove it. If you want it on the resume, show it in a career note at the bottom of the Hiring managers and recruiters have short attention spans and have no desire to read a multiple page resume that includes every job the person ever had. Instead, less is more when it comes to your resume. If it's not relevant remove it. Job seekers may think their entire job history will get them the position, but hiring managers are largely interested in the information that pertains to the current job opening. If you still want to list these jobs, you can show them as part of a "career note" at the bottom of the employment history section of your resume.

I am often asked how far back a resume should go. I advise clients that 10 or 15 years is usually sufficient because it is more recent. There are times, however, where older experience can be relevant, and you may want to "highlight" that job that can be referred to as "Highlighted Experience." If it is out of the 10-15 year range, I recommend that you do not date it. This technique worked for me when I wanted to highlight an experience that was 30 years old but did not want to "date" myself. It is that 30-year-old job that got me an appointment as a Career Counselor for the City University of New York.

Myth 6: Provide a detailed list of your duties for each position

Employers do not care about every detail of your previous job. I find a tendency toward this among IT professionals, government workers, academics, and engineers, but they are not the only "offenders." The only thing hiring managers want to know is how you can contribute to their company and relevant projects that demonstrate your ability to perform.

Myth 7: Social media is the best way to network and get a job.

Social media sites have made it easier to make connections with people in your industry. The most effective way to get a job is not via social media or the resume but face-to-face meetings and communication. Professional associations can put you on the radar screen, as can other networking events that put you in front of someone who can help you get the job. Don't discard social media and be mindful that recruiters will look for you on LinkedIn, Facebook, or other platforms because it's easy to do so.

Myth 8: Only paid experience counts.

Any experience that is paid or unpaid can be valuable and should be added to the experience section of your resume. This becomes more critical if you have been out of the workforce for some time or don't have a long job history. If volunteer experience is related to the role you are seeking, this could be the lynchpin to getting the job. At the very least, it can demonstrate your passion for the work you do.

5

Organizing Your Job Search

When you are ready to start your job search, it is time for reflection about your career. Do you want to remain in your industry, or do you want to try something new? The "one size fits all" resume will not work for you if you are open to change.

At this stage, your focus should be on research. Before you start, think through what you want from your next job and beyond that. I speak from personal experience. A big chunk of my career was in the private sector at the executive level. I was in the engineering and construction industry. There came a time when I didn't want to be in this industry anymore. Although I was successful in the boom and bust periods of this industry, I had enough and was ready for a change. I was also nearing retirement and was thinking about what I might do after giving up the nine to five grind.

A Personal Job Search Journey

I had gone to college to study to be a social studies teacher. Despite a degree and a license to teach, fate took me elsewhere. First to the Department of Labor, where I became an Employment and training specialist for federal grant programs. Somehow, I wound up on the business side of construction and engineering. I had taken a job in Mayor Koch's office where I was managing a job training in the construction program. I eventually moved on to be a contract administrator for construction with a billion-dollar state agency and later I moved to the private sector, where I grew smaller companies into bigger ones.

I finally decided to come full-circle in my career and become involved in employment and training. Now I had to find out what types of jobs suitable for me. I was always at the executive level, and now I decided to uncomplicate things and just work one on one with people. I started to review job boards. My favorite source was Indeed.com because I was easily able to search out different job titles, read up on employers who were hiring, go to their websites and look at their career pages. Long story short, I gained an understanding of what they were looking for, and my resume was not going to cut it. That's when I started to dive into resume writing. I was desperate to remake my five-page resume. The first job I applied for was as a Job Coach, working with individuals with disabilities for a non-profit agency. Next, I applied for and got a job with the City University Research Foundation, where I was a Career Counselor for a federal jobs program for about four years. By the time I retired, I had my next move figured out. Become a Certified Professional Resume Writer and work at home in my pajamas.

Launching Your Job Search...Network or Job Board?

You have many options in taking advantage of the Post-COVID-19 job market to find a new or better position. Should you work on your professional network or spend time on job board sites. My recommendation is to do both.

While personal interaction can achieve strong results, perhaps even better than responding to ads posted online, there are advantages to online applications if you have a level playing field.

It is beyond the scope of this book to dive into the art of networking and branding by establishing your blog or website to establish your brand.

Job Boards & Search Engines

A job board is a single website that contains up to thousands of job postings that are searchable for job seekers. These are job aggregators that can identify jobs worldwide, including career sites, employer job listings, and other job boards. These job boards have search engines much like Yahoo and Google.

There are many different job sites, and many of them provide a range of tools to help candidates in their job search. This may be in the form of blog posts, articles, videos, prospective employer ratings, and salary ranges.

These are some of the top Job Boards and Search Engines being used today:

Indeed.com is the number one job search site today. You can search jobs by location, keyword, or employer name, and Indeed links you to the employer's job posting on their sites. Indeed.com is user-friendly, and I recommend using this site.

LinkUp.com is very similar to Indeed, except that job listings are indexed directly from company career sites instead of other job board listings.

Glassdoor.com can be very helpful. It is unique from others because it provides ratings of prospective employers by current and former employees. Employees also share benefits and salary information, and this is good for you to know, especially if you have lined up an interview with one of them.

Jobrapido.com allows you to search jobs by job title and geographic location, listing over 20 million jobs monthly and recording 55 million hits per month. It is the second-largest global job aggregator and is headquartered in Milan but conducts business in 58 countries.

Monster.com and CareerBuilder.com each used to dominate the job search industry. They continue to help with resumes and advice, and function as job engines.

Some other search engines and job boards include *StartJobs.com, JustJobs.com, Trovit, Jobs, SimpleTelecommute, and JobCase.*

Job Hunting Survival Guidance in the COVID-19 Era

COVID-19 has brought local, state, and federal government mandates, turmoil in the financial markets, and disruptions in our way of life. Many job applicants fear that they cannot find a job during this chaotic time of rapid changes. As we start to emerge from COVID-19, we can already see that companies are still operating and still need qualified candidates. Some employers are ramping up to hire. There is no doubt that the hiring process is longer than it used to be, so be as patient as you can be. Consult the job aggregator websites described above. Work your network to find out what is going on with your contacts and their employers. Think about your transferrable skills, especially if you have decided to make a career change. We are still very much a service industry, with job growth expected in Grocery, Warehouse, Delivery, and Health Care.

Many companies, because of social distancing, are doing business remotely, and remote work opportunities are everywhere. This is good news if your skills allow you to work this way from your home. In my practice, most people working remotely are in technology-based, marketing, sales, and creative positions.

Now is a time to inventory your skills and add to them. If you use the job boards and search engines with any frequency, you will gain valuable insight into the types of skills employers are looking for. If your skills do not match the skills that employers advertise in their job postings, your resume will simply not work for you, regardless of who writes it. There are ways to add to your skillset without investing much or any money. Many of my clients have added skills to their resumes through self-study online. For example, LinkedIn offers thousands of courses at a low monthly subscription rate, as does Udemy.com. There are others as well. You can list the certifications you receive from enrolling and add keywords from your resume. You can learn hard and soft skills and take credit for them. Most job postings are searching for these keywords. As I wrote earlier, keywords come from experience, education, and training.

6

The Resume Building Process

Let's build a hypothetical resume! I am going to take you through the process that I follow as a certified professional resume writer when I am working with clients. Over 93% of my clients, according to a "scorecard" that I receive from a national resume service that I write for, have job interviews within three months, leading to a positive employment outcome.

Step One:

- Decide what your target is. Clients often tell me that they want a resume before they start their job search. I don't advise this approach because it won't work for them. If you just want a pretty resume, but not effective. But if you want a resume that gets results, you need to do a little homework.

- Identify job postings that represent the Job vacancy that you want to apply for. Based on my experience as a resume writer, if I select 10 similar job postings from a source like Indeed, Monster, and/or Company websites that post vacancies, I will find that there is generally commonality in all of these job postings. A good job posting has these parts to it:

  - A description of the company and its branding statement.
  - A profile of the kind of candidate they are looking for.
  - Keywords that are listed that speak to qualifications, functions, and skills. These keywords will be used in an ATS scan of your resume to score it in terms of most to least qualified.

The following sections of your new resume should be informed by the job postings you have identified as "of interest" in applying for vacancies. These are the HEADLINE, PROFILE, and CORE SKILLS sections of the resume (refer to the Hybrid Resume illustration in Chapter 2).

The HEADLINE is what you put on the resume that identifies you as a qualified candidate for the advertised position. If you are qualified for this role or have worked in this type of position, I recommend you put the job posting title as your Headline.   Ditch terms like "Career Profile, Career Summary, or Executive Summary, and banish the words "Career Objectives" from your resume.

When you style the resume with the target position, you immediately make it easier to get the hiring manager's attention. You are sparing the manager from hunting and pecking through your resume to see if it warrants further review. What you have done is focused the reader and aligned your resume to the position in question. When you use generic terms, your resume has no focus at first glance.

A word about "Career Objective". This is old-school, out-of-date verbiage that does not belong on a post-COVID-era resume. Why? Simply because it tells the reader what YOU *want*, but doesn't tell the reader what you bring to the table.

When you write your Profile at the very top of your resume, you should be answering the question any employer has: "Why should we hire you?" In three or four sentences, make your case and show them that your career matches the profile they have described in the job posting.

Step Two:

Analyze as many job postings for your target position as possible and list the keywords that represent skills that you have. You need to be comfortable with what you list because you may be asked to defend it, so if you list it, give thought to why this belongs on your resume. While it is true that resumes are scored by keywords, be as ethical as possible.

This is an important point. Clients often ask me why I am recommending certain keywords. First off, if they are not familiar with something I listed in the draft, even after I explain it, it comes off the resume. When I do resume workshops, I tell clients:

- If you learned skill in school or a training program, list it on your resume. This does not mean that you are an "expert" but that you have some level of competency in the skill, meriting inclusion on your resume.
- If you acquired the skill on the job, list it on your resume. Once again, you may or may not be an expert but if you can speak to it, list it. It very well may get you in the door, and then you can explain this on your resume.

Step Three:

Write the profile within the framework of the ads that interest you. Oftentimes, the employer will describe who the ideal candidate is, and use "soft skills" or "transferable skills" that can apply to any job. It's easy to find. Look for terms like "team player", "resourceful", tenacious". "team player", "cross-functional relationships", "relationship builder" and so on.

Now I want to take you through the process that I follow for my clients. Following is an actual Job Posting that I pulled from Indeed.com. I will show you how I build a resume around this job posting:

Project Manager – New York City School Construction Authority - Various School Construction Projects

Acme Constructors
Queens, NY 11101
Employer actively reviewed candidates 4 days ago

Job details

Salary $80,000 - $135,000 a year
Job Type Full-time
Number of hires for this role 10+

Qualifications

- Bachelor's (Preferred)
- Construction Experience: 8 years (Preferred)
- Project Management: 4 years (Preferred)

Full Job Description

Company Overview

Acme Constructors is a Construction Management (CM) firm founded in 2000, specializing in the construction and renovation of educational, municipal, cultural, residential and transportation construction projects for public sector government agencies. AC serves as the owner's representative and advocate through all phases of a project and under a variety of delivery methods. Active primarily in the North East Region, where the company was formed, AC has spent the last 20 years building a diverse project portfolio that includes work in New Jersey, New York, Connecticut, and Pennsylvania.

Project Description

AC is managing construction on various NYC SCA school construction projects in New York City five (5) boroughs. The Projects include and are not limited to: new construction, exterior and interior renovations, new boiler systems, exterior masonry restoration, window replacement, roof replacement, green roof infrastructure, flood elimination, electrical upgrades, and HVAC refurbishment.

Responsibilities and Duties Responsibilities and Duties

- Oversee all daily field operations to ensure proper site safety, construction, progress, quality control, housekeeping, and daily log;
- Provide guidance, leadership and direct supervision of contractors and site staff;
- Management of schedule, including weekly preparation of 2-week look ahead;
- Proactively schedule and coordinate all contractors to ensure completion of the project in accordance with the project schedule and to ensure that no additional costs are required for completion of work;
- Develop comprehensive understanding of project strategy and commitments including financial goals, scheduling, logistics, phasing, milestones, and inspections;
- Ensure assigned Jobsite operations are in compliance with design/specifications, completion on schedule, within budget and to quality standards;
- Demonstrate and maintain effective and open dialogue with the project team regarding changes in work, job conditions, contractor relations and any deviation in the direction of the project;
- Work in partnership with our client and contractors to maintain an updated and accurate project schedule that reflects the changes in project status and that meets the cost and time requirements of the project;
- Run weekly meetings, including project and contractor meetings;
- Manage the RFI process; consisting of the creation of and suggestions on solutions to site issues and tracking them through closeout;
- Maintain and review punch list process to ensure all are addressed and executed in a timely manner;
- Manage closeout process and review punch list process to ensure all are addressed and executed in a timely manner;
- Continuously promote positive contractor relations by dealing professionally and fairly with

a **Qualifications**
- Bachelor degree in engineering/architecture, and/or construction related field from an accredited college or university.
- 8 years experience in as a technical specialist in construction and design related field.
- 4 years must have been involved in managing all phases of construction work.
- Or a comparable combination of education and experience.
- Shall have the ability to understand and interpret contract documents such as specifications, drawings and shop drawings.
- Shall have experience in new and renovation type construction.
- Must have a valid drivers license.

Let's extract keywords from the posting" that should be on your resume if you are applying for this position by each section of the job posting:

Project Description

AC is managing construction on various NYC SCA **school construction projects** in New York City five (5) boroughs. The Projects include and are not limited to **new construction, exterior, and interior renovations, new boiler systems, exterior masonry restoration, window replacement, roof replacement, green roof infrastructure electrical upgrades, and HVAC refurbishment.**

Keywords from this section:

School Construction, New Construction, Exterior/Interior Renovations, Boiler Systems, Exterior Masonry, Window Replacement, Roof Replacement, Green Roof Infrastructure, Electrical Upgrades, HVAC.

Job Summary

The ideal candidate is a Construction Project Manager experienced and responsible for scheduling the work, overseeing school construction, maintaining the **schedule, site safety, coordinating communication** between the school and the contractor, **closeout** of projects, including **payments** to contractors.

Keywords from this section:

Scheduling, Site Safety, Project Communication, Project Closeout, Contractor Payments.

Responsibilities and Duties

- Oversee all daily field operations to ensure proper **site safety, construction progress, quality control, housekeeping, and daily log.**
- Provide guidance, leadership, and direct **supervision** of contractors and site staff;
- Management of **schedule**, including weekly preparation of 2-week, look ahead;
- Proactively schedule and coordinate all contractors to ensure completion of the project per the project schedule and to ensure that no additional costs are required for completion of work;
- Develop a comprehensive understanding of **project strategy** and commitments **including financial goals, scheduling, logistics, phasing, milestones, and inspections**;
- Ensure assigned Jobsite operations comply with design/specifications, completion on schedule, within budget, and to quality **standards**;
- Work in partnership with our client and contractors to maintain an updated and accurate project schedule that reflects the changes in project status and that meets the cost and time requirements of the project;
- Run weekly meetings, including project and **contractor meetings**;
- Manage the **RFI process**; consisting of the creation of and suggestions on solutions to site issues and tracking them through closeout;
- Manage **closeout process** and review **punch list** process to ensure all are addressed and executed promptly;

Keywords from this section:

Site Safety Oversight, Field Operations, Contractor/Staff Supervision, Scheduling, Project Strategies, Logistics, Project Phasing/Milestones, Inspection, Quality Standards. Contractor Meetings, Project Closeout, Punchlist.

Qualifications:
Bachelor's degree in engineering/architecture, and/or construction-related field from an accredited college or university.
8 years experience as a technical specialist in the construction and design-related field.
4 years must have been involved in managing all phases of construction work.
Or a comparable combination of education and experience.
Shall have the ability to understand and interpret contract documents such as specifications, drawings, and shop drawings.
Shall have experience in new and renovation type construction.
Must have a valid driver's license.

Keywords from this Section:

Degree (Engineering, Architecture, Construction Management), Design, Construction, Project Management, Drawings and Specifications, Shop Drawings. New Construction, Renovations, Driver's License.

Composite List of Keywords Posted for this position:

School Construction	Site Safety
New Construction	Project Communication
Exterior Renovations	Project Closeout
Interior Renovations	Punchlist
Boiler Systems	Contractor Payments
Exterior Masonry	Field Operations Oversight
Window Replacement	Contractor/Staff Supervision
Roof Replacement	Project Strategies
Green Roof Infrastructure	Project Phasing/Milestones
Electrical Upgrades	Inspection Services
HVAC	Quality Control/Standards
Project Scheduling	Contractor Meetings

This job poster is looking for candidates that possess these core skills as represented in keywords used throughout the job posting. How many resumes do you suppose this poster will see that lists all of these in keywords somewhere in the resume? Maybe one out of 10 or maybe none out of 100. This gives you a competitive edge. If your resume contains all of these keywords throughout your resume, whether the employer eyeballs your resume or scans it through ATS tracking systems, given a level playing field, you are in the game. Strategically, I would place the most important of these keywords within the top one-third of page one of your resume. I suggest that you place most of these words or phrases in the Core Skills Section of your resume, directly under the Career Profile section.

Remember what I said before: the average HR professional or hiring manager will not invest more than six seconds in scanning your resume before they decide whether to read it. I think this approach would get this particular job poster's attention. I also will venture to guess that if you look at ten other similar postings, you will find some if not all of these keywords in those too. There may be a few others that apply to you and in that case, add them to the list, and then send your new resume to all of them and see if this approach is working for you. I am betting your resume will get some attention.

Now, let's work backward up to the Headline and Profile Section of your resume. First the Headline: Here are two possibilities that come to mind: School Construction Project

Manager (Best), Construction Project Manager. There is no reason why you can't add a **Branding Statement** right under the Headline. Here is an example:

SCHOOL CONSTRUCTION PROJECT MANAGER

Proven Ability to Deliver Projects on Time, On Budget, Safely, and With Quality

Next, let's put the Profile Section together. Remember, this is replacing the old school Objective Statement and presents a value proposition to the employer. It answers the question, "Why Should We Hire You"? If we look at the following section of the job posting, we will find some clues that will help us answer that question.

Qualifications
• Bachelor's degree in engineering/architecture, and/or construction-related field from an accredited college or university.
• 8 years experience as a technical specialist in the construction and design-related field.
• 4 years must have been involved in managing all phases of construction work.
• Or a comparable combination of education and experience.
• Shall have the ability to understand and interpret contract documents such as specifications, drawings, and shop drawings.
• Shall have experience in new and renovation type construction.
• Must have a valid driver's license.

Here is what I come up with, working from this job posting. If I was doing this resume for an actual client, I would have additional insights that could influence how I would write it.

JAMES JAMESON, CCM

Walden Pond, MA | 718-123-4567 | JamesJCCM@yahoo.com

SCHOOL CONSTRUCTION PROJECT MANAGER

Proven Ability to Deliver Projects on Time, On Budget, Safely, and With Quality

Certified construction project management professional with more than eight years of experience in construction and architectural design, with a focus on the new construction and rehabilitation of schools and institutions. Experienced in managing all phases of the construction project life cycle from bid and award through project closeout. Recognized for saving $1 million in claims or change orders by identifying inconsistencies and inaccuracies in plans and specifications and recommending value engineering solutions.

Core Skills

• Exterior Renovation	• Interior Renovation	• HVAC/Boiler Systems
• Window Replacement	• Green Roof Infrastructure	• Electrical Upgrades
• Project Schedules	• Contractor Payment Processing	• Construction Inspection
• Quality Control	• Project Execution Strategies	• Contractor Meetings

With the example above, I have provided a portion of an ATS-friendly resume section. This is approximately 1/3 of page one of the resume. The balance of the resume will consist of the job history, education, certifications, technology skills, and other pertinent information.

BUILDING THE JOB HISTORY SECTION OF YOUR RESUME

This section should continue to brand you as someone who will bring value to the organization. The accounting of your work history should not be a restatement of various job descriptions. While it is important to give the employer a sense of context for what you have done, it is equally important to demonstrate accomplishments that you have brought to previous employers.

Almost every resume includes an array of job duties performed in past positions. Accomplishment statements, on the other hand, can help set your resume apart by explicitly narrating what you've achieved in your career. They go beyond solely explaining what your job responsibilities were. Most hiring managers already have a firm grasp on the duties associated with varying roles anyway. What they're looking to learn is how well you performed them.

Accomplishments show three things:

1. The precise actions you took in a given situation
2. The skills and abilities you used when facing a challenge
3. The results that you achieved

As you seek to identify your accomplishments, it can be helpful to ask yourself the following questions:

- Have I received awards, special recognition, or a promotion?
- Have I developed a new system or procedure?
- Have I identified and resolved a problem that others didn't see?
- Have been involved in a team effort that produced a specific result?
- Have I reduced cost or increased revenue?
- Have I helped others achieve their goals through my leadership?
- Have I helped improve communications or relations between groups?

Determine the skills that are required of the positions you're seeking within your industry; with those in mind, consider all the times you overcame high-pressure circumstances, achieved financial goals, made efficiency improvements, showcased your leadership skills, or generally exceeded expectations. If you can apply those experiences to the skills your prospective employers are seeking, those are perfect examples to highlight as accomplishment statements on your resume.

How to Identify Accomplishments for your Resume:

- **Challenge** – What was the existing problem, need, or situation?
- **Actions** – What did you do about the challenge?
- **Results** – What outcomes did you produce?

Once you've identified which accomplishments to highlight your resume can be focused less on your job duties and more on what you accomplished. This is how you show your value to an employee. As shown in the examples above, accomplishments can contain quantitative measurements and tangible results, or be more qualitative, showing how you implemented processes, trained staff, or developed process improvements that improved the organization.

- Start your statements with impactful language, such as <u>action verbs</u>.
- Use quantitative measurements when you can, emphasizing on tangible results.
- Focus only on skills and experiences that are relevant to the job you're seeking.

BLAND RESUME STATEMENTS VS. ACCOMPLISHMENT-DRIVEN EXAMPLES

<u>Original Statement on Resume</u>	<u>Accomplishment-Driven Version</u>
Increased customer satisfaction as customer care representative.	Maintained a 97% satisfaction rating over 24 months, contributing to a 50% increase in revenue.
Responsible for managing inventory and maintaining appropriate stock on hand.	Reduced time spent on inventory by staff by 35% by reorganizing and centralizing physical storage.
Showed properties to potential home buyers.	Conducted an average of 20 real estate showings per week on upscale properties valued between $800,000 and $3 million.
Served drinks to customers with a friendly-upbeat demeanor.	Increased lounge revenue by 25% within three months by cultivating a loyal customer base.
Supervised trainers in delivering fitness training to gym members	Built memberships and revenue by establishing performance goals for the department and driving the team to meet performance and customer service standards.

Took over the supervision of the Hardware Team and revamped procedures to improve operations.	Inherited a lack of organization and structure within the Hardware Team and revamped organization, reporting, and tracking systems, improved time for fulfillment of equipment requests.
Inspected food establishments in non-compliance with sewer ordinances.	Implemented an education program for local food establishments in non-compliance with Town sewer ordinances, reducing food safety violations.
Processed shipments to customers and coordinated with manufacturers.	Overcame shortages in supply by meeting with customers to prioritize deliveries and with manufacturers to review their production schedules, allocated supplies from longer lead-time orders.
Improved customer satisfaction by responding to their needs.	Maintained a 97% satisfaction rating over 24 months as a customer care representative
Served as event planner, administering and managing the company's program for prospective customers.	Directed 35 events annually, with more than 20,000 attendees by utilizing a social media and targeted email campaign.

RESUME ACTION VERBS

Avoid the same tired words to compose the bullet points and statements in the Job History section of your resume. Instead of words like *Led, Handled, Managed, Responsible For…*, try some of these or other alternatives to describe those functions:

Led team in…

Consider these:

Chaired	Executed	Orchestrated	Planned
Controlled	Headed	Organized	Produced
Coordinated	Operated	Oversaw	Programmed

Developed, created, introduced…

Consider these:

Administered	Designed	Established	Engineered
Built	Devised	Formulated	Launched
Charted	Founded	Pioneered	Spearheaded

Increased efficiency…

Consider these:

Accelerated	Delivered	Maximized	Capitalized
Advanced	Expanded	Stimulated	Furthered
Boosted	Expedited	Enhanced	Outpaced

Changed or improved:

Consider these:

Centralized	Integrated	Refocused	Modified
Converted	Overhauled	Influenced	Redesigned
Customized	Redesigned	Transformed	Remodeled

Managed a Team….

Consider these:

Aligned	Enabled	Inspired	Mobilized
Directed	Guided	Mentored	Shaped
Facilitated	Fostered	Motivated	Unified

Communicated….

Consider these:

Authored	Composed	Counseled	Promoted
Briefed	Conveyed	Advocated	Publicized
Co-Authored	Convinced	Persuaded	Defined

Achieved Something…

Consider these:

Attained	Awarded	Earned	Outperformed
Exceeded	Succeeded	Surpassed	Reached
Targeted	Demonstrated	Recognized	Completed

Let's finish building James Jameson's resume:

Here is the resume strategy used in responding to this ad:

1. I determined the profile of the candidate that the poster was looking for. The candidate needed at least eight years of experience in construction or design, school construction experience, a four-year degree, or a combination of experience and education. I drew on this when writing the Profile.

2. I highlighted and listed all of the keywords that I could find in the ad, assuming that the resume will be scanned by ATS software to score the resume. Even if the resumes are reviewed manually, I am capturing attention within the six-second window by the way I have styled this.

3. My Profile presents a value proposition that presents credentials, education, and related experience and an example of the value that was delivered in the previous position.

4. The work history (one job position is presented for illustration) are value-driven statements. In this case, some representative project experience is added that is very related to the job being applied for.

If you are writing your resume, you should be prepared to spend four or five hours on the initial resume if you follow my recommendations for building a resume. While this seems like a lot of effort, consider this...you will only need to tweak this resume for similar positions in the future.

JAMES JAMESON, CCM

Walden Pond, MA | 718-123-4567 | JamesJCCM@yahoo.com

SCHOOL CONSTRUCTION PROJECT MANAGER
Proven Ability to Deliver Projects on Time, On Budget, Safely, and With Quality

Certified construction project management professional with more than eight years of experience in construction and architectural design, with a focus on the new construction and rehabilitation of schools and institutions. Experienced in managing all phases of the construction project life cycle from bid and award through project closeout. Recognized for saving $1 million in claims or change orders by identifying inconsistencies and inaccuracies in plans and specifications and recommending value engineering solutions.

Core Skills

- Exterior Renovation
- Window Replacement
- Project Schedules
- Quality Control

- Interior Renovation
- Green Roof Infrastructure
- Contractor Payment Processing
- Project Execution Strategies

- HVAC/Boiler Systems
- Electrical Upgrades
- Construction Inspection
- Contractor Meetings

Professional Experience

New York City School Construction Authority   2010 - 2021
Construction Project Manager

- Saved $250,000 by value-engineering proposed design and providing alternative methods of construction.
- Executed project strategies by developing a project roadmap and work breakdown structure for each new operation, delivering the project three months ahead of schedule.
- Directed subcontractors in working safely within occupied facilities, resulting in no OSHA-recordable safety incidents.
- Proactively managed contractor project schedules in each phase and at each project milestone identified potential obstacles to completion and drove resolutions.
- Successfully defended against a $1 million claim by presenting documentation demonstrating that contractor non-compliance was a result of the delay.

Representative School Construction Projects:

- New Addition, Public School 188, Brooklyn ($3.5 million)0.
- New Construction, IS 270, Corona ($19 million)
- School Weatherization, All Boroughs ($6 million)
- School Rehabilitation, Exterior/Windows, Newark ($10 million)

Education
B.S., Construction Engineering Technology, Chandler University

Certifications
Certified Construction Manager (CCM), Construction Management Association of America
OSHA Certification – 30 Hours, 10 Hours

Technology Summary
MS Project, MS Word, MS Excel, AutoCAD, Timberline, Primavera P6, BIM

Strategy used to build James' resume in response to the job posting:

- Determine the profile of the candidate the poster is looking for.
- Capture keywords representing skills and experience being sought.
- Write a value proposition at the top of the resume along with a headline that captures the attention of the employer.
- Write a work history using action verbs and demonstrating accomplishments that have brought value to previous employers.

This may seem like a lot of effort in creating a resume for a specific job posting but consider this:

- Once you have this draft, use it as a "default" for that position.
- If you apply to other *similar* jobs, all you need to do is to "tweak it" or adjust it to add or remove some keywords, perhaps change the Headline to the job title posted.
- It will still give the job poster the impression that you understand who they are looking for and why you might be a good fit.

7

Job Winning Resumes that Work

This chapter contains some of the best examples of resumes the follow the principles outlined in this book. These examples are for different occupations across a range of different industries and maybe a helpful reference. Resume samples are filed alphabetically by occupation/industry:

I am providing samples of resumes that I have written for clients within the last three years. There is a broad sample of resumes by occupation and industry. On the average these resumes have resulted in interviews with prospective employers and 90% of the clients that I furnished these resumes to were employed within three months. Each resume contains keywords that were obtained by researching job postings for that exact position.

Selected Occupations/Industries:

- Advertising – Digital
- Account Executive
- Accounts Receivable
- Architect - Building
- Business Analyst
- CPA
- Construction Manager
- Drafter
- Engineer – Structural
- Footwear Designer
- Food Service – Cook
- Food Service – Wait Staff
- Facilities Manager
- Finance Manager

- IT – Data Program Manager
- IT – Network Engineer
- IT – Software Engineer
- IT – Software Developer
- IT – Systems Analyst
- Maintenance Manager
- Office Manager
- Operations Manager
- Sales Manager
- Recent Graduate
- Supply Chain – Warehouse
- S.C. – Distribution Specialist
- Teacher
- Technician – Medical Lab

Matthew Cagney

516-777-5242 | Matt.Cag@gmail.com | www.linkedin.com/in/matthew-cagney-9952a129/

DIGITAL MEDIA STRATEGY PROFESSIONAL

Experienced producer, audio engineer, and project manager with an entrepreneurial spirit in providing leadership and problem solving skills to promote quality audio content in a collaborative team environment. Manage podcast services designed to reach targeted audiences and advertising strategies that resonate with millennial, Gen-X, Gen-Z and Boomer consumers. Apply story-telling and creative skills to develop the finished product. Manage the production process from concept to final audio mix and digital presentation. Sound editorial judgment and sophisticated audio production skills.

- Editorial Skills / Direction
- Storytelling
- Targeted Audiences
- Attention to Detail
- Social Media Management
- Digital Editing
- Music / Audio Mixing
- Social Media Advertising
- Promotional Strategies
- Guest Bookings
- Podcast / Radio Production
- Content Writing
- Topic Research
- Audio Sharing Platforms
- Audience Engagement

Key Qualifications

- Take ownership and overall responsibility for creative, top priority initiatives from concept to delivery.
- Provide hosts and producers with guidance for big picture arcs and develop weekly prep sheets for show recordings.
- Research ideas for programming and edit content on a range of subjects.
- Manage the branding of the subscriber broadcast channels, overseeing production of live and recorded talk shows
- Deliver engaging, intelligent, and entertaining programming that appeals to the target audience.
- Collaborate with marketing and advertising digital, interactive, ad-sales and public relations teams to build and promote the brand to the target demographic.

Professional Experience

Cyclone Media   2019 – Present
Web Content Producer / Founder
Established a full service production company focused on developing unique web content and content videos for marketing for Podcast companies and entrepreneurs launching new ventures.
Developed the company mission statement that draws on the talent of producers, cinematographers and editors to create unique and buzzworthy videos, podcasts and web content for the brand through turn-key solutions.
Produced, host and engineer podcasts and establish distribution channels and social media strategies.
Set up channels for podcast distribution and required technical support.

Museo Media Group, New York, NY   2017 - Present
Senior Producer
- Supported the launch of a Podcast advertising service for Fortune 100 companies for media company that produces compelling, upbeat, authentic content directed to millennial audiences.

MATTHEW CAGNEY – Page 2
516-777-5242 | Matt.Cag@gmail.com

- Create and build a strategy around voice for GMG brands including, PureWow and ONE37pm.
- Conceptualize and create custom audio content for Fortune 100 companies
- Connect clients to the targeted consumer demographic by taking opportunities in the audio space.
- Create content around advertising, reversing the traditional approach to advertising.
- Leverage social media to build consumer trust for clients serviced by the Gallery Media Group.
- Create shows, hire talent, develop content, and implement audio strategies.

STARBRITE RADIO | New York, NY
Producer / Associate Producer, Entertainment Weekly Radio | 2014 – 2017
- Strategically utilized social media and audio sharing platforms to build audiences and promote programming for channel.
- Produced unique programming including "Off the Books", an acclaimed program focused on the art and book publishing hosted by Entertainment Weekly editor Tina Jordan, and produced various programming focused on eclectic pop culture.
- Coordinated production of shows that included "Obsessed!", "Entertainment Weirdly", "Behind the Scenes" and "Press Play" featuring various formats including call-ins, interviews with entertainment luminaries and music-focused programming.
- Produced live-audience special events – "EW Town Halls" featuring top Hollywood "A-Listers" and the recap show for Mad Men, Outlander, CW superheroes, Pretty Little Liars, WestWorld, The Editor's Hours, Press Play, and Inside Movies.
- Scripted, produced and recorded the EW Radio's hourly news updates.
- Performed highly diversified tasks across pre-production, production, and post production.
- Worked with other producers and programming team to create superior EW branded programming.
- Supported creative processes, content development, and production, with creative and technical abilities.
- Produced image for programming including promos to promote shows.
- Developed novel, creative ways to represent content and obtained/edited audio materials for production.
- Ran audio board for various live and taped programming and determined proper sound element mix.
- Ensured that the on-air product was up to broadcast standards.

EDUCATION

B.A., Radio and Audio, Emerson College
Media Arts | Sound Design | Dimensions of Creativity | Media Arts Production | Interactive Media | Sound Analysis | Writing + Concept Development | Audio Production | Location Sound Recording

Technical Skills and Social Media Platforms

Adobe Audition | Pro Tools | Prophet NexGen Digital System | Media Touch | Millennium Radio Systems | Digital Audio Console Mixing Board | Master Control Operations | TV Studio Operations | Mac OS X and PC Operating Systems | MS Office Suite | Twitter | Instagram | Facebook | YouTube | Vimeo

ALEXANDER JOHNSON

Phone: 555.222.2222 ▪ Email: alexjohn@gmail.com

ACCOUNT EXECUTIVE

Program, project, and customer management professional with more than ten years of experience in leadership roles with managers and global teams. Drive adoption of Ariba Networks and applications. Proven experience with business process transformation and change management implementation. Experience with cloud services implementation and deployment. Strong understanding of best business practices and alignment with spend management. Work at the expert level, partnering with executive leadership to improve network competencies and transfer knowledge to customer engagement professionals. Consistently meet and exceed account-specific revenue and profitability targets.

─── CORE STRENGTHS ───

- ✦ Ariba Network Deployment
- ✦ C-Level Relationships
- ✦ Customer Program Performance
- ✦ Global Deployment Methodology
- ✦ Complex Customer Engagement
- ✦ Customer Relationship Management
- ✦ Profit & Loss

- ✦ Account Management
- ✦ Business Case Drivers
- ✦ Project Management
- ✦ Team Management
- ✦ Account Penetration
- ✦ Forecasting
- ✦ SLA Performance

- ✦ Supply Chain
- ✦ Supplier Enablement
- ✦ Business Transformation
- ✦ eBusiness
- ✦ HRI Management
- ✦ Workforce Diversity
- ✦ Business Transformations

─── PROFESSIONAL EXPERIENCE ───

SPROCKETDRIVE   2016 - Current.
CUSTOMER ENGAGEMENT EXECUTIVE

- Work at the expert level, developing partnerships for geographic and strategic area customers, developing, and improving Network competencies and knowledge transfer to Customer Engagement Executives.
- Prepare forecasts, devise account penetration, and customer engagement plans, delivering business outcomes.
- Diagnose customer business opportunities, analyze business case drivers, identify program risks, and establish action plans improving CCO business processes associated with communicated network value propositions.
- Collaborate in the development of quarterly plans improving Spend adoption and SMPP yields for the portfolio.
- Engage with key decision-makers and executive sponsors and participate in quarterly account review meetings.
- Increase spend under management, network adoption, transaction volume and trading relationships on the Network, track SLA performance, and overall customer satisfaction.
- Recognized for meeting and exceeding account-specific revenue and profitability goals for account portfolio.

ALEXANDER JOHNSON- Page 2

SLUDGE DIRECT ENERGY – Woodbridge, NJ   2014 - 2016
SUPERVISOR – SALES SUPPORT

- Led regional proposal and contract generation process by supporting sales teams and customers. Managed customer relationships by proactively addressing customer inquiries, assisting with high-level issues.
- Achieved continuous sales process improvements by collaborating with other regional sales and support leaders to achieve continuity in sales processes across commodities.
- Trained, mentored, coached, and supervised a team of up to 20 in meeting performance objectives within the business strategy, and process training for new and current team members.
- Ensured team compliance with internal policies and business rules.
- Worked collaboratively to streamline processes that define task responsibility and accountability.
- Developed, enhanced, and maintained key reporting elements for Sales Support East.
- Contributed support in the development and implementation of the CRM integration project.

DINO ENERGY CORP. – Wyomissing, PA   2013 - 2014
SALES COORDINATOR

- Learned market dynamics associated with prospecting and sale of DR, Oil, Natural Gas, and Electricity.
- Prepared proposals and generated contracts with a high degree of accuracy for immediate processing. Identified and qualified prospects for the field sales team.
- Met and exceeded sales program metrics for new and renewal rates and margins by maintaining and retaining accounts through relationship building and excellent sales support services.
- Successfully identified, developed, and closed sales prospects for all products sold in assigned region.
- Performed pricing analysis, incorporating cost and rate reviews to demonstrate cost savings to customers and maximizing business relationships.
- Managed local consultants and sales agents and the coordination of responses to the RFP that generated new business.

EDUCATION

Master of Business Administration, Project Management
Keller School of Management, DeVry University, Philadelphia, PA, 2011 GPA 3.98/4.0

Bachelor of Science, History
East Stroudsburg University, East Stroudsburg, PA

ADDITIONAL INFORMATION

- Sigma Beta Delta International Honor Society, Keller Business School of Management
- Customer Service Certified
- Beta Be Me Fraternity President
- Greek Academic Award
- Eagle Scout

Melissa Tinderbaum

Henderson, NY | 845-444-1213 | Mtinderbaumyahoo.com

Accounts Receivable Analyst / Administrative Support Specialist
Data-driven, fact-based, detail-oriented approach to analysis and problem-solving.

Accounts Receivable professional enhancing the organization's ability to complete the collection process by applying strong analytical research and resolution skills. Articulate, negotiating payments in a customer-facing position with all levels of the accounts payable management chain without compromising positive business relationships. Identify and resolve billing and payment issues to minimize loses. Support the organization with strong administrative skills, including managing heavy client interaction, bids and proposals, and financial reports.

Core Competencies

>> Generally Accepted Accounting Principles	>> Accounts Receivable
>> Bookkeeping and Payroll Processes	>> Billing & Collections
>> Superior Attention to Detail	>> Invoicing / Reconciliations
>> General Ledger Reconciliation	>> Cash Flow Analysis / Financial Controls
>> Aged Receivable Management	>> Customer Service / Customer Relations
>> Negotiating / Influencing	>> Financial Reports / Forecasting
>> Contract Bidding / Proposals	>> Schedule Management
>> Payroll / Time & Attendance	>> Office Management

PROFESSIONAL EXPERIENCE

BARRONS, INC. – Danbury, CT   2006 – Present
Administrative / Accounts Receivable Assistant
- Generate invoices for the Repair Department of Roofing Contracting firm and oversee the credit and collections process while managing diverse administrative functions in a fast-paced environment.
- Research billing history of accounts to resolve client issues.
- Track the company's ability to cash in on outstanding invoices, mitigating risk and improving cash flow.
- Apply research and analytical skills to investigate issues and ensure that action is taken for resolution.
- Initiate contacts with customers to collect on delinquent payments.

Accomplishments:
- Reduced aged receivables by strengthening the tracking of payments and by exercising influencing and negotiating skills with clients while maintaining positive relationships.
- Mitigated risk of penalties by proactively ensuring compliance with DEP and State regulations for underground tank maintenance and documentation.
- Avoid overpayments and underpayments by ensuring that time and attendance records are properly submitted for payroll.
- Accepted project management responsibilities during the spinoff of a new company, ensuring that systems and operations ran smoothly during an intense period of transition.
- Reduced shipping cots by 50% by changing shipping processes.

F&G HOSPITALITY CONSULTING, INC. – Tampa, Fl   2006 – Present
Consultant / Office Manager
- Directed office operations and maintained effective communications with clients for firm supporting hospitality clients in hotel operations, finance, marketing, sales, food and beverage operations, spa and golf operations, casinos and entertainment venues.
- Accountable for quality assurance reviews of reports and deliverables issued to clients.
- Efficiently organized and managed travel arrangements and schedules for consultants.
- Managed correspondence, incoming phone calls, and first class mail and package deliveries.

Accomplishments:
- Acted as an in-house consultant to call hotels and locations to collect data used to generate Quality Assurance reports based on interactions with facility employees, enabling more meaningful reporting to clients.
- Stepped in to take over accounts receivable functions due to a shortage of office personnel, enabling the company to maintain positive cash flow.

RIVEL RESEARCH GROUP – Westport, CT   2005 – 2006
Research Analyst / Reception
- Managed office administrative tasks and compiled research reports for consulting firm delivering factual, data-driven intelligence used by management and boards to mitigate risk and improve company valuation.
- Compiled research reports and drafted presentations based on data analysis.
- Edited outgoing client reports, sales letters, and materials for quality and consistency.
- Assisted Research Director in developing questionnaires used for various research projects.
- *Accomplishments:*
- Developed the core data set used for all company research projects, including coding and tables.
- Increased client satisfaction by editing reports improving the quality of deliverables to a more professional standard.

EDUCATION

- **Bachelor of Science Degree – Business Administration**
  Southern New Hampshire University, Happytown, NH
  > Financial Accounting, Managerial Accounting, Business Statistics, Corporate Finance, Business Information Systems, Business Policy, and Strategy

CERTIFICATIONS

- Notary Public, State of Connecticut

TECHNOLOGY SUMMARY

- Sage Timberline, DataForma, DoForms, Adobe Acrobat
- MS Office: Word, Excel, PowerPoint, Outlook, Access

ROBERT WALDON, R.A.

Pompano Beach, FL | 123-456-7890 | jwaldon123@gmail.com

LICENSED ARCHITECT

Professional Architect with a Master's degree in Architecture and more than ten years of experience designing commercial buildings, offices, and residential homes. Proven ability to provide designs that achieve design intent while remaining within the project budget established by the Owner. Experience in design of publicly-funded infrastructure. Approach design with accuracy and superior technical skill. Thrive in a fast-paced environment, applying strong organizational and problem-solving skills.

CORE SKILLS

Building Codes | Specifications | Model Making | Drafting | Project Management | Budgeting | New Construction
Renovation | Interior Design| Architectural Programming | Quality Assurance | Tenant Build-Out | Value Engineering
School Construction | Correctional Facilities | Construction Services | Submittals Review & Approval | Punch List

TECHNICAL SKILLS

BIM, AutoCAD, Revit, MS Excel, MS PowerPoint, MS Word, MS Outlook

PROFESSIONAL EXPERIENCE

SR. ARCHITECT | ABC Design Consultants | Fishkill, NY | 2015 – Present
- Provide technical leadership, guidance, and assistance to development teams in the implementation of established architecture and design.
- Meet deadlines for deliverables by creating, designing, and developing solutions, and coordinating with engineering teams to ensure constructability and consistency.
- Provide best-fit architectural solutions for an average of ten projects annually with budgets ranging from $5 million to $30 million, defining scope and sizing of work.

Accomplishments:
- Revamped design procedures by introducing standardized design protocols to address inconsistencies in the development of drawing and specifications, and compliance with design protocols of government agency clients.
- Participated in value engineering sessions that saved $3 million for a $30 million budgeted project by recommending solutions requiring alternate materials and construction methods.

ARCHITECT | ABC Design Consultants | Fishkill, NY | 2015 – Present
- Prepare project estimates and architectural plans based on preliminary inspection of existing structure and conditions and implementing architectural processes to complete projects.
- Meet with client to determine policies and procedures and develop preliminary program requirements and planning to meet the needs of the Owner.

Accomplishments:
- Received recognition by firm for ability to develop client relationships that have led to an additional $3 million in architectural fees.

EDUCATION & LICENSES

- Harvard University, MA in Architecture, 2015
- City College, City University of NY, B.A. in Mathematics, 2010
- Registered Architect – New York, New Jersey

Savannah Walsh

sawa2011@gmail.com | (555)-727-2716 | Dry Gulch | Texas

Business Analyst

A versatile member of the IT project team performing the roles of requirements specialist, test leader, and project manager. Successfully build relationships to learn requirements, understand business processes, document use cases, and translate business requirements into systems solutions. Develop solutions addressing a wide range of problems, applying technical knowledge, concepts, and theories in recommending the best systems approach.

Core Competencies

Stakeholder Business Requirements	Software Development Life Cycle	System Troubleshooting
Business Needs Analysis	Business Use Cases	Testing
SQL Data Queries / ETL	Software Technology Implementation	Project Management
Data Analysis	Business Process Improvement	Cost Control
Voice of the Customer	BI Tools	User Training
Functional Specifications	Process Modeling	Agile/Scrum

Technology Summary

Programming Languages:	SQL
Databases:	MS Access, Oracle (SQL Series), DB2
Reporting Tools:	Crystal Reports 8.0
Operating Systems:	MS-DOS, Windows 95/98,/NT/2000/XP, Apple McIntosh, Linux
Software:	MS Office: Word/Excel/Access/PowerPoint/Outlook, MS Visio, Rational Rose, Rational Requisite Pro, Adobe Acrobat, FrontPage, Lotus Notes
Performance Testing Tools:	Virtual User Generator, Load Runner
Processes/Technologies:	Rational Unified Process *RUP), Waterfall, UML, SharePoint 2007
Automation Tools:	Requisite Pro, Win Runner, QTP, Test Director, Quality Center

PROFESSIONAL EXPERIENCE

National Oscilloscopes | Sep 2015 - Current

SYSTEMS ANALYST

Assess and analyze system needs working with stakeholder business and IT teams to develop system requirements and solution designs, working in an Agile environment. Derive requirements based on data analysis.

- Elicit and document requirements from internal customers and stakeholders.
- Align new proposed capabilities to business priorities, best practices, policies, and standards.
- Use SQL for data extraction, analysis, and modeling for process analysis.
- Define system, data, process, and automation requirements based on business requirements
- Designed Process Flow Diagrams and web page mock-ups using MS Visio.
- Managed schedules and collaborated with different teams working on the projects.

SAVANNAH WALSH – Page 2

sawa2011@gmail.com | (555)-727-2716 |

Systems Analyst/National Instruments - Continued
- Develop and execute test designs and plans to validate solution
- Develop and deliver system setup and system training documentation for system and process changes
- Coordinate SDLC activities as a Scrum Master for a product team.
- Used Jira for ticket management and collaborated and provided solutions.
- Developed checklist and guidelines for R&D team to improve alignment of new product development with existing processes.
- Resolved inherited system with data issues caused by faulty business rules and system failure by analyzing root causes and providing solutions technically and through process changes.

⚑ Great Western Life | Jan 2010– Aug 2015

BUSINESS ANALYST
- Gathered business requirements by interviewing business users, stakeholders, and Subject Matter Experts, and performed in-depth data analysis. Elicit, mine, and document business rules and processes.
- Prepared Business Requirements Document and used Relational RequisitePro to manage, analyze, and convert business requirements into functional specifications.
- Developed use cases from requirements and created UML use case, activity, and sequence diagrams.
- Designed Data Flow Diagrams, Entirety Relationship Diagrams, and web page mockups with Rational Rose and MS.
- Coordinated project schedules and issued project progress and status reports to management.
- Used SQL to extract data for process analysis and modeling.
- Inherited project to add several product lines for new Customer group, working with Marketing and Legal to align different products that had legal bindings to purchase or receive services, meeting company deadlines in three months.
- Worked on data analytics project enabling Actuarial department to design new products that met company requirements and generated revenue, coordinating with all stakeholders during design that resulted in a well-coordinated platform for different teams, within six months.

EDUCATION & CERTIFICATIONS

- Master of Science, Engineering – Winnipeg Technologies University, Canada
- Bachelor of Science, Environmental Engineering, John Walsh University, Duluth, MN

Brenda K. Ferrone, CPA

01N241 Hazelwood Road | Saint Cloud, IL 60145
Mobile: 630-777-2000 | Email: ferrone.brenda.k@outlook.com

CERTIFIED PUBLIC ACCOUNTANT

Senior financial professional with thirty years of proven ability to lead and manage the finance function, delivering the whole spectrum of financial support for futures commission merchants, trading firms, and family office managing multiple and diverse businesses. Support management by implementing an effective control environment and developing policies and procedures. Manage the maintenance of accurate books and records in accordance with tax, company policy, and statutory regulations. Self-starter approach to work and problem-solving, detail orientated, highly organized and motivated to deliver business process improvements.

https://www.linkedin.com/in/brenda-ferrone-27b41929

Highlights

- Financial Statements
- Management Reporting
- General Ledger
- Accounting Process Improvement
- Audit Program Management
- Regulatory Compliance/Reporting
- Accounting Controls

- Budgeting
- Staff Training / Development / Supervision
- Variance and Account Analysis
- Reconciliations
- Accounting Policies and Procedures
- Consolidated Reporting
- Tax Compliance

Professional Experience

AXE Group of Companies / AXE Chicago LLC   2008 – Present
Privately owned international group of companies.
Controller

- Complied with U.S. reporting requirements for Futures Commission Merchants (FCMS) including daily seg and secured, capital comps and monthly 1FR).
- Coordinate completion of international corporate tax returns, 5472s, FBARs, and VAT reporting.
- Direct accounting system functions including general ledger.
- Manage daily, monthly, and yearly accounting functions for 40+ companies and entities.
- Prepared annual budgets and analyzed cost variances for business groups.
- Primary contact and coordinator for external financial audits in six countries.

<u>**Brenda K. Ferrone, CPA – Page 2**</u>

- Create financial analysis and reporting that supported important business decisions for acquisitions, liquidations, and reorganizations.
- Prepare monthly consolidated statements for all entities with five different functional currencies.
- Supervise, train, direct, and mentor staff in local and international offices.

Accomplishments:

- In the absence of a CFO, took on CFO-related responsibilities for over 10 years.
- Consulted for analysis of major restructuring and funding issues, reporting to the owner.
- Maintained single accountability for all accounting functions over a 10-year period.
- Transitioned London accounting department to Chicago to reduce redundancy and cost.
- Introduced new financial and management reporting system for the new family office investment group of 40+ international entities.
- Established new accounting office in Singapore and trained new staff on department procedures.
- Reduced audit timing by implementing preset requirements that were standard across all global entities for reports and reconciliations.
- Tested and evaluated general ledger systems to ensure that business needs were met, saving the company the cost of a full system conversion and implementation.

Rodney & Rivak, Inc., Chicago, IL   2000 - 2008
New York Stock Exchange listed broker dealer and futures commission merchant with $30 million in equity.
Division Controller/Senior Accountant
Prepared and presented monthly divisional income statements and related analysis to senior management. Directed staff accountants in preparation of daily segregated and foreign secured statements. Instrumental in implementing new multi-currency general ledger system.

Britebart & Stone, Chicago, IL   1998 - 2000
Chicago Board of Trade office of public accounting firm that specialized in audits of broker dealers, futures commission merchants, and funds.
Senior Associate
Planned, audited and filing regulatory and financial reports. Reviewed systems of internal controls and made recommendations to client management.

Accreditation

Certified Public Accountant

Education

Northwestern University – Evanston, IL – B.A. Accounting

EDWARD T. TAYLOR, SR.

Braintree, MA 02703 ▪ C: 555-123-4567 ▪ Email: ett123@gmail.com

BUILDING CONSTRUCTION PROFESSIONAL

Construction Project Manager and sustainable solar energy installations, recognized for improving construction practices, means, and methods, and for ensuring quality, safety, and building code compliance during construction phase operations. Local Inspector certifications. Complete knowledge of building construction, fire prevention, light, ventilation, safe egress, and other building practices to ensure the safety and comfort of building occupants. Competency in application state and federal regulations and standards for building inspection. Seeking to leverage skills and experience for a Building Inspection/Code Enforcement role.

CORE SKILLS

▪ Project Management	▪ Quality Control	▪ OSHA/Regulatory Compliance
▪ Quality Assurance	▪ Inspection Reports	▪ Environmental Health & Safety
▪ State Building Codes	▪ Blueprint Readings	▪ Building Ventilation Systems
▪ Construction Inspection	▪ Construction Plans	▪ Fire Protection Systems
▪ Building Construction Supervision	▪ Zoning Restrictions	▪ ADA Compliance
▪ International Residential Code	▪ NFPA Sprinkler Code	▪ NFPA Fire Alarm Code

EDUCATION & LICENSES

- Bachelor of Science – Business Administration/Management – Bryant College, Smithfield, RI
- Hoisting & Hydraulics Operator
- Construction Supervisor's License (State of MA)
- Local Inspection Exams 1A, 1B, and 3B (Passed: Certification Pending)

PROFESSIONAL EXPERIENCE

PROJECT MANAGER ▪ **Webb & Boyd Construction** ▪ **Seekonk, MA** ▪ **2012 – Present**
- Supervise large scale custom residential subdivisions and condominium construction.
- Schedule contractors and ensure adequate resources for completion of construction project milestones.
- Perform material takeoffs for lumber and materials for custom homes.

Accomplishments:
- ✓ Took over 50 unit condo project with cost overruns and scheduling delays, designed new workflow processes and timelines for required selections from customer, and completed remaining 80% of the project on time and on budget.
- ✓ Resolved supply chain issues by devising new logistics plan with suppliers for material receipt and a resulting 10% discount on materials.

OWNER ▪ **21st Century Solar** ▪ **Braintree, MA** ▪ **2000- 2012**
- Operate full-service residential and commercial Solar PV installations, including design of system, permitting, engineering, construction, and commissioning of the system.
- Oversaw design and installation of residential and commercial rooftop systems, residential ground systems, dual-axis solar trackers, solar carports, and array upgrades.

Accomplishments:
- ✓ Successfully managed and delivered over 75 photovoltaic projects.
- ✓ Developed and implemented audit programs to demonstrate the benefits of conversions.

EMIL ORTIZ

2025 Flatbush Avenue |Brooklyn, NY 11223 | 123-456-7890 | EmilCADop@yahoo.com| www.linkedin.com/in/Emil/

AUTOCAD DRAFTER

More than 12 years of experience developing architectural designs using AutoCAD, with extensive knowledge of structural, mechanical, and electrical design techniques. Experience with residential and commercial construction projects, and proficient in AutoCAD and Autodesk Mechanical (2D). Excellent understanding of dimensioning, scaling, the development of building plans.

CORE SKILLS

- Drafting Practices & Procedures
- Plan Edits & Modifications
- Site Data Collection/Field Visits
- Project Survey Data Analysis
- Structural Layouts
- Blueprints/Sketches
- Quality Assurance
- Design Coordination
- Building Codes

TECHNICAL SKILLS

BIM, AutoCAD, Revit, Civil 3D, MS Excel, MS PowerPoint, MS Word, MS Outlook

PROFESSIONAL EXPERIENCE

AUTOCAD DRAFTER | ABC Design Consultants | Fishkill, NY | 2013 – Present
Serve as resource for design staff as it pertains to drafting practices and procedures.

- Utilize AutoCAD Civil 3D and related engineering software packages to complete assignments on time and within Atwell standards.
- Ensure compliance and acceptance of documents by complying with standard drawing procedures and design protocols.
- Achieve accuracy in data for design development by visiting construction sites to measure field dimensions.
- Provide technical guidance to less experienced personnel on large and small scale drafting projects.

Accomplishments:

- Spearheaded project to upgrade office software to improve the integrity of drawing and reduce production time, enabling on-time completion.
- Network with outside users of software, keeping current on issues and making recommendations for improvement.

EDUCATION

Associate Degree in Drafting

James Woods Technical Community College, Marion, NC

WALTER CHEN, P.E.

Union City, CA | 765-123-9876 |chenw2@gmail.com | https://www.linkedin.com/in/chen-walter-pe36ba0a126/

STRUCTURAL ENGINEER

- Licensed Professional Engineer specializing in structural engineering, and skilled in developing relationships with government and industry clients leading to additional projects and company growth.
- Experience conducting forensic investigations using advanced field investigation techniques. Strong command of fundamental structural engineering principles.
- Proven ability to lead and execute structural engineering and mentoring junior staff in project engineering and project management roles.
- Recognized by leadership as a driven project manager, deftly leveraging project resources and demonstrating the ability to quickly learn and adapt to new challenges.

Core Skills

Forensic Investigations • Effects Modeling • Structural Evaluations • Project Management
Structural Failure Analysis • Plans & Specifications • Quality Assurance • Project Scope/Estimates
Structural Engineering • Remediation Design • Conditions Inspections • Project Schedules
Depositions/Trial Testimony • Building Codes • Independent Research • Mentoring/Training

PROFESSIONAL EXPERIENCE

Project Engineer
Heidemann Consulting Engineers | San Francisco, CA | Jul 2018 - Present

- Member of select team of engineers conducting rigorous data-based approach to developing risk mitigation strategies for clients with multiple security challenges, ensuring suitability of design and integrity of solutions.
- Lead blast hardening design, physical security, and risk mitigation for new and existing government-owned entities for agencies including DOE, DOD, GSA, and VA, and for private infrastructure projects.
- Conduct nonlinear dynamic analysis of facilities and infrastructure subjected to explosive effects, and vulnerability assessments for high-profile Federal facilities.
- Deliver performance-based design solutions for long term facility planning.

Highlights:

- ▶ Managed Explosive Safety Siting and Anti-Terrorism Force Protection planning for safe manufacturing operations for a confidential DOD operations facility, leading to award of seven additional projects from client.
- ▶ Delivered blast hardening, progressive collapse, and vehicle ramming design for new $1.4 million world class terminal and major transportation hub at Newark International Airport.
- ▶ Proposed a progressive collapse mitigation and structural blast hardening for new private high rise 800 foot Tower at Transbay Terminal, San Francisco

DESIGN ENGINEER
W.T. Grant. Ltd. | Bangalore, India | Jul 2014 – Jul 2016

- Supervised a cross-functional business team of five members, coordinating and planning project requirements with internal team and clients.
- Project manager for planning and executing the project lifecycle and meeting all project milestones.
- Provided cost estimates, allocated project resources, issued project schedules and updates, and established milestone due dates.

WALTER CHEN, P.E. - Page 2
765-123-9876 |chenw2@gmail.com

Design Engineer-W.T. Grant, Ltd. - Continued
Highlights:

- ▶ Determined adequacy of structural members for 100 year old, high skew (70°) Crumlin River Underbridge, UK, and reduced re-construction costs by 25% by providing alternate solutions in consultation with stakeholders.
- ▶ Developed a tool to expedite the work for the design of various types of structures, including single and double cantilever and portal frames for supporting overhead line electrification systems for the MMLE Overhead Line Electrification Light Structures in the UK.
  - Developed Overhead Line Electrification (OLE) Design Tool for semi-automated structural design allowing cross-functional teams to input data for physical properties, loading conditions, support conditions, embankment, and clearance conditions, providing output to size structural elements.
  - Increased agility and productivity of team, enabling Rail business to win more contracts and increasing business revenue by 20% in 2015 – 2016.

COMPUTER SKILLS

- **Structural Analysis**: RAM Elements, RAM Connections, SAP 2000, STAAD. Pro, Abaqus, Structural Bridge Design software (SAM), TEDDS, LUSAS, HILTI Profis, Micro Station
- **Blast Analysis**: Wingard, ConWep, ConBlast
- **Computer-Aided Design**: AutoCAD, SketchUp, Revit • Programming: C, C++, Python, MATLAB, Mathcad

EDUCATION

- **Master of Civil Engineering –** Purdue University | West Lafayette, IN **|** May 2015
- **Bachelor of Civil Engineering –** Chandler University | Chandler, AZ | Jun 2013
- **Coursework:** Advanced Steel Design, Advanced Structural Mechanics, Bridge Engineering, Concrete Technology, Environmental Engineering, Estimating/Costing, Fluid Mechanics, Hydrology/Water Resource Engineering, Irrigation Engineering, Materials & Construction, Pavement Design, Reinforced Concrete Design, Project Management

LICENSES

- Professional Engineer – State of California – License # 92058 – Expires Mar 2021

ADDITIONAL INFORMATION

Affiliations:

- American Society of Civil Engineers (ASCE

Jim Wright

⌂ New York, NY 10027 ✉ jwshoedesign @me.com ☎ 646-888-0001
in www.linkedin.com/in/jimw-r-1ba8a42/

Senior Footwear Designer

Exploring the potential, pushing the limits of design, combining point of view and problem-solving to build the next era of footwear.

Outstanding Senior Footwear Designer, managing the product development life cycle from conceptualization to manufacturing to achieve world-class performance. Utilize feedback and teamwork to improve and push the limits of design. Nurture the design narrative and hit deadlines and key calendar dates.

Key Qualifications

- ▶ Leverage a great sense of style and understanding of emerging trends, styles, and consumer demand to lead seasonal storytelling, color direction, and material development.
- ▶ Flexible team player with solid communication skills, acceptance of different views, and valuing inclusiveness.
- ▶ Strong sense of footwear product creation process and timeline.
- ▶ Expertise in technical footwear manufacturing processes, rapid prototyping and 3-D model making processes.
- ▶ Footwear-specific experience in the sports products industry.

Core Competencies

Design Concepts | Technical Package Development | Creative Presentation | Seasonal Storytelling
Functional Styling | Product Manufacturability | Project Management | Design Process Management
Market Research | Fashion Trends | Consumer Demand | Design Protocols | Material Design | Sales Support
Color Theory/Direction | Mass Market & Private Label | Product Price Points | Digital Design Platform

Technical Skills

Adobe Illustrator ▪ Adobe Photoshop ▪ Sketch Artis ▪ Designer ▪ Sketchbook Pro ▪ MS Office Suite

PROFESSIONAL EXPERIENCE

◤ FREELANCE FOOTWEAR DESIGNER - CONTRACTOR | 2008 - Present

- ▪ Apply knowledge of color and materials to footwear design, creating CAD and material drawings of new design and updates of existing design.
- ▪ Manage seasonal brand direction, market research, trend insight, and business requirements to select materials and present new innovative concepts true to the brand.
- ▪ Drive multiple projects through the product development life cycle, develop and review prototypes, and execute timely technical and design packages with a high detail and accuracy level.
- ▪ Work with clients' marketing teams to develop tech packs and develop technical sheets.
- ▪ Successfully design most categories of shoe design at all price points and market sectors, specializing in women's, men's children's, casual dress, athletics, and athleisure shoes.
- ▪ Design women's and men's footwear using Nike Air and Lab technology.

JIM WRIGHT – PAGE 2

FREELANCE FOOTWEAR DESIGNER | 2006 - 2007

- Applied style sense, creativity, and problem-solving to the product design process, delivering color and materials solutions to meet consumer demand for athletic footwear.
- Created seasonal storytelling, color direction, and material development to support seasonal business strategies and consumer preferences trends.
- Consistently met go-to-market dates and project milestone deadlines in producing functional, stylistic designs.

FOOTWEAR DESIGN MANAGER | 2003 - 2006

- Developed footwear concepts with a focus on men's and women's Kenneth Cole and REACTION lines.
- Created decks of design trends and research for team review, working with design team to build color and material library and create seasonal mini walls.
- Managed creation of presentations for design team requirements, including virtual sketches and virtual trend reviews.
- Worked closely with merchandising for line sheet creation for targeted markets.
- Managed the sample development cycle and ensured on-time delivery of sales samples
- Created and supported team relationships by sharing information and ideas with others.

SENIOR FOOTWEAR DESIGNER – FRYE BOOTS & CO. | 2002 - 2003

- Executed concept development, market research, collection calendars, and merchandising plans.
- Implemented design and brand direction for the upcoming season.
- Spearheaded specification development, prototype assessments, construction requirements, and pre-production functions, including quality control.
- Developed relationships with manufacturers and suppliers and collaborated to launch men's and women's footwear and the Small Frye kids product line.

SENIOR FOOTWEAR DESIGNER – VITA SHOES | 2001 – 2002

- Created concept designs from the initial design stage to final presentations and sample production, supporting the product team with mood boards, tech packs, and sample revisions.
- Maintained and updated design sketches and tech specs, researched materials, and collaborated with the product team to share design and development feedback.
- Worked under guidance of Senior Footwear Designers to create or refresh designs that reflected Adidas's design philosophy and inspire targeted customers.
- Executed design projects by researching consumer/athlete and market needs based on design briefs.

EDUCATION

Illustration & Design & Fashion Design | Fashion Institute of Technology

John Smith
123 Apple Tree Parkway | Cherry Lane, PA
555-456-789 | jsmith@gmail.com

Line Cook

Dedicated, punctual line cook skilled in food preparation and completion of portions of customer orders, working various stations. Diversified experience in grilling, baking, broiling, sautéing, and salad making. Team player, focused on excellent customer service, food safety and quality. Excellent communication skills in busy, noisy environments. Proven ability to work under pressure. Capable of reading and understanding basic cooking procedures.

Key Skills

Food Safety & Sanitation | Knife Skills | Soups & Sauces | Sautee/Grill/Broiling | Cleaning/Sanitizing
Steaks & Chops | Salads | Inventory Control | Team Work | High Productivity

Work Experience

Line Cook | Bourbon Street Grill | Minneapolis, MN | 2015 - Present
- Assist the Head Chef in preparing and serving food items
- Prepare all food items in a timely and hygienic manner
- Follow recipes and food presentation specifications as set by Main Street Grill management
- Introduced new popular menu items that increased revenue during "specials" nights.
- Implemented safety and sanitation program, resulting in "A" rating from a "C" rating from the Department of Health.

Cook's Helper | Apple Cider Inn | Duluth, MN | 2012 - 2015
- Stored food items and maintained the highest levels of sanitation and cleanliness
- Replenished raw food, garnishes, and other ingredients to serving lines
- Assisted in serving lines and prepared simple foods, including salads and soups

Education
Merriweather High School
High School Diploma

Scott Brown

San Francisco, CA   scottyb@gmail.com   415-222-1234   www.linkedin.com/in/scottyb/

Director of Facilities

Passionate facilities operations professional with more than eight years of experience managing commercial and residential properties that include multiple story high rise buildings to historic landmarks. Recognized for dedication, the ability to build high-performing teams. Contribute to client retention, new business development, and organizational growth. Great communicator, good listener, collaborative, and empathetic, thriving in a diverse, multi-cultural environments.

- Continuous Process Improvement
- Cost Reduction
- Allocation of Resources
- Human Resources
- Energy Information Systems
- Security Systems
- Building System Optimization

- Space Programming
- Vendor Management
- Electrical/Lighting Systems
- Conditions Assessments
- Component Life Cycle
- MEP System Optimization
- Safety/OSHA Compliance

- Fire/Life Safety Systems
- HVAC/Boiler Plant
- BAS
- Commissioning
- Training
- Building Codes
- Quality Assurance

PROFESSIONAL EXPERIENCE

GOLDEN ARCHES NATIONAL PARKS CONSERVANCY –Salt Lake City, UT | Sep 2019 - Present

FACILITY MANAGER

- Oversee 14 buildings and grounds across three counties, including several historic buildings and maintain newly build LEED-certified buildings.
- Managed $3.2 million operational budget and control the allocation of funds.
- Work with cross functional department leaders to develop appropriate budgets for capital construction and maintenance projects.
- Direct large custodial accounts including COVID-19 sanitation and disinfection program.
- Supervise maintenance of a 66 vehicle fleet, including GSA-furnished vehicles.
- Ensure performance of subcontractors and vendors comply with contract requirements.

Highlights:

- ► Led the COVID 19 reopening team in implementing special projects, following guidance from the CDC, the State, the City, and the County.
- ► Created strategic safety guide outlining reopening during pandemic, signed by all business partners, providing a roadmap for safe operations during this health crisis.
- ► Procured and installed a new GPS tracking system and new fleet management software to improve the tracking of assets and staff and ensure scheduled maintenance.

PENINSULA ISLAMIC COMMUNITY CENTER – Los Angeles, CA | Nov 2018 – Sep 2019

PRINCIPAL/OWNER

- Planned and implemented construction and redevelopment projects and secured agency approvals.
- Managed, maintained, and replaced building systems, aquatic center, fitness center, systems, and public spaces including grounds.

Highlights:

- ► Implemented the first safety training program in five years for Facilities staff, dramatically improving overall safety performance during onsite operations.

EDUCATION

B.S. Construction Management, City College of New York

Art Buchman

Dublin, MA | (555) 357-7774 | artieb123@yahoo.com| https://www.linkedin.com/in/matt-b-5b62b26/

Finance Manager

Recognized by leadership and colleagues as a standout, consummate financial partner with the proven ability to analyze and large, complex issues, and achieve efficiencies and cost savings in operations. Reliable leader, teacher, and mentor building high-performing teams. Strength in data analysis, maximizing return on investment, and relationship building. Experience across a range of business areas, including media, technology, operations, budgeting, and forecasting. Strong communicator with ability to work independently and collaboratively in a team environment.

Core Competencies

Financial Planning & Analysis (FP&A) | Forecasting | Investment Portfolio Management
Financial Statements | Product/Segment Profitability | Return on Investment (ROI) | Ad Hoc Financial Reports |Marketing & Sales | P&L
| Benefit Analysis | Budgets |Process Improvement |Supply
Accounting Practices | Cashflow Modeling

Professional Experience

Director – Financial Planning & Analysis (Technology) | Jul 2015 to Apr 2020
Safeway Auto Glass | Timberlake, OH

- Managed IT investments and expenditures for a company with over $2B in annual sales, developed budget and 18-month rolling forecasts, placed controls on spending, and implemented policies and procedures that improved profitability.

Accomplishments:

- Inherited IT Department that was operating overbudget by $2M and required a transformation.
- Reduced capital expenditures over three consecutive years, from $40M to $20M by creating monthly P&L statements and variance reports for leadership to drive ownership of issues, built financial forecasts, and annual budget.
- Implemented a spending policy and process for the IT department, changing a process that enabled procurements without input from Finance, Procurement, and PMO, eliminating unapproved spending and ensuring expenses did not exceed technology spend budget.

Manager – Financial Planning & Analysis (Marketing) | Feb 2011 – July 2015
Safeway Auto Glass | Timberlake, OH

- Analyzed investments on a $60M marketing campaign and helped facilitate media strategies for optimized media spend aligned to market conditions, managing $100M for the Marketing Team.
- Created long-term benefit analysis to support $150M spend in traditional media over seven years.

Accomplishments:

- Analyzed initial investment in TV advertising with a $7M investment, increasing to $35M annually by developing daily, weekly, and monthly reports, giving leadership confidence to continue investments, elevating company brand, awareness, and consumer preferences.
- Developed long-term analysis to measure digital and traditional media investments of $50M, using ten years of data, and recommended continued investments, building market share and record-breaking revenue.

ART BUCHMAN – PAGE 2

Senior Analyst – Financial Planning & Analysis | Oct 2009 – Feb 2011
Safeway Auto Glass – Timberlake, OH
- Provided budget and forecast for Marketing team, managed payroll, research, and expenditures.
- Developed monthly variance analysis, annual budget forecast, and P&L for Wholesale Organization, reporting $100M.
- Created annual payroll budget for 4,000+ field technicians.

Accomplishments:
- Managed company's first significant investment in traditional media for $20M TV and radio spending.
- Maximized payroll efficiency by creating monthly variance reports for store leaders.

Analyst II – Financial Planning & Analysis Development | Sep 2007 – Oct 2009
Acme Door Mats | Columbus, OH
- Managed monthly commission payment for 250 sales representatives.
- Provided management with balance sheet budget, forecast, and cash flow modeling to guide business planning.
- Developed a $400M budget and forecast for Supply Chain team, ensuring ownership of the budget, cost control, and profit maximization.

Senior Analyst – Telecom (Telecommunications & Network | Jun 2005 – Jun 2007
Acme Door Mats | Columbus, OH
- Created 18-month rolling forecast and $50M budget for Telecom and Network Teams and managed telecom and network budgets for 500+ store locations.
- Performed financial analysis for Requests for Proposal for major contract renewals with AT&T, Sprint, Avaya, and Call Recording.
- Managed the monthly close process and financial reporting.

Telecom Analyst – Telecommunications | Jun 2000 – Jun 2005
Martin Auto Interiors | Columbus, OH
- Developed a $30M budget and forecast for annual Telecommunications spend and reported monthly to leadership.
- Managed capital budget for $10M spend and provided ROI to determine value of capital improvements.

Accomplishments:
- Obtained over $1M in cost reductions by auditing telecommunications spend and implementing changes.

Technical Skills

AS400 | Oracle Financials | Oracle ADI | Microsoft Office | Agile | Advanced Access | Advanced Excel | Business Objects | IBM Mainframe | IBM TM1 | Clarity PPM

Education & Training

Bachelor of Arts| University of Toledo | Toledo, OH

Harry Feldstein

Columbia, MD 21045 | Feldstein357@hotmail.com | 202-222-00101

IT Data Program Manager

Passionate about the power of data in driving business operations and growth.

IT professional with 25+ years of experience in data and system management leadership. Provide the leading edge by evangelizing a data-driven culture that enables process improvements. Strive for higher levels and productivity, taking full ownership of project planning, reporting, and risk mitigation and ensuring successful delivery across all workstreams. Build high-performing teams, providing mentorship for professional development.

Core Competencies

- Data Program Management
- Database Design
- Data Storage & Protection
- Cross-Functional Team Leadership
- Data Management
- Business Requirements/Solutions
- Software Development
- Process Improvement
- Vendor Management

- Metadata Development
- Data Quality
- Data Governance
- Strategic Metrics/Scorecards
- Data Strategy Implementation
- Data Development
- Project Management
- Spatial Analysis
- Systems Administration

Technology Summary

Software Tools:	SQL Developer, AutoCAD, Microsoft Office, Intergraph CAD, ArcGIS 10.X Desktop, ArcSDE, Pictometry, Google Earth, GeoMedia, Microsoft Access
Data Transformation Tools:	Informatica, FME, ORACLE, CopyStorm, StreamSets
Systems Integration:	Salesforce, Intergraph CAD 911, Remedyforce, PowerPlan, Peoplesoft, QuickBase, PASS (DC procurement system), Microsoft SharePoint
Analytics/Database Platforms:	MicroStrategy, Tableau, Python, ArcGIS, ESRI Open Data, Hadoop, Hive, Elastic Search, Oracle, SQL Server, GitHub

PROFESSIONAL EXPERIENCE

STATE OF MASSACHUSETTS – Boston, MA   2010 – Present
DATA CURATION & PROGRAM MANAGER
Managed a $1 million budget and ten-member team upon promotion from GIS Data Team Lead.
Engaged system team to document, investigate, and monitor data warehouse infrastructure and benchmark performance .Collaborated cross-functionally with applications, analytics, systems, and operations teams and customers to identify and integrate information supporting analytics, reporting, and mapping services.

Accomplishments:

- Converted outdated manual processes to a new automated methodology that increased processing capability by 75%.
- Improved data processes, governance, and strategic initiatives, following CMMI Institute Data Management Maturity model that applies a structured framework of data strategy best practices, building customized roadmap for data management maturity.
- Enabled an enhanced security framework for the data program by evaluating software and developing and presenting technical requirements and management solutions.

LEE J. WILLIAMS

Union City, NJ 08427 | 732 222-3456 | Email: LeeJ5@outlook.com

SENIOR NETWORK ENGINEER

More than 25 years of experience in troubleshooting Network and Application related issues. Skilled in packet capture for processing and intercepting/logging traffic, decoding raw data from data streams, and analyzing content to identify and resolve issues. Self-motivated, dedicated to customer service, meeting project deadlines, and building and supporting high-performing teams. Leverage advanced computer and network systems knowledge to deliver creative solutions.

HIGHLIGHTS

Network Design & Development ▪ Customer Communications ▪ Security Administration ▪ Testing
QoS for VoIP ▪ System Implementation ▪ Network Routing Protocols ▪ Complex Issue Troubleshooting System Maintenance Wireless Controllers ▪ Firewalls ▪ VPN Administration ▪ Performance Tuning

TECHNICAL SKILLS

Sniffer Pro, Distributed Sniffer Detection System, Infinistream Appliances, nGeniusONE™ Service Assurance Platform, Border Gateway Patrol, OSPF Routing Protocol, Enhanced Interior Gateway Routing Protocol (EIGRP), Cisco ISR9000, ISR4300, ISR4400 integrated services series routers. Cisco ASR1000 ASR9000 WAN routers, Cisco Catalyst 3650, 3850, 4500 and 9000 series switches, Catalyst 6500 series switches, Nexus 9000, 7000, 5000 and 2000 in the Datacenter Cores, CISCO PIX Firewalls, ASA Firewalls, Cisco TACACS+ Assess Control Protocol, Cisco Router Platforms, Nortel Passport 6400, Window OS, Sun Solaris, HP UNIX, Meraki MX, MS and Z3's devices, Meraki dashboard

PROFESSIONAL EXPERIENCE

SENIOR NETWORK ENGINEER   2004 - Present
Liberty Mutual Insurance

- Provide support to troubleshoot network problems, install and maintain hardware and software infrastructure, including firewalls, routers, switches, and wireless controllers according to policy and best practices.
- Deliver third level support for sizeable worldwide network with 15,000+ nodes.
- Worked on the following devices:
  - → Cisco 800, 1800, 2800, and 3800 integrated services series routers. Cisco 7200, 7300, 7600, ASR1000 WAN routers and Cisco Catalyst 2960, 3560, 4500, and 4900 series switches.
  - → Catalyst 6500 series switches, Nexus 7000, 5000 and 2000 in the Datacenter Cores
- Supported worldwide MPLS networks managed by large carriers such as Verizon, AT&T, and British Telecom.
- Supported a large global point to point VPN network and hundreds of LAN's in remote offices.
- Performed troubleshooting of routing protocols with BGP, OSPF, and EIGRP.
- Applied knowledge of VoIP and QoS configurations and Cisco wireless.
- Security Administrator for Cisco Checkpoint firewall, Cisco PIX, and ASA firewalls, and Cisco TACACS+.

Highlights:

- ✦ *Deployed global resolution to complaints of network slowness after deployment of Cisco 3850 switch stacks by providing a switch configuration change for 100MB Avaya phone system affecting performance.*
- ✦ *Resolved overnight fails of DMZ batch jobs by using NetScout Infinistream to capture and analyze event and correct issue with a Palo Alto Firewall.*

LEE J. WILLIAMS 732 222-3456 | Email: LeeJ5@outlook.com   Page 2

EARLIER EXPERIENCE

Senior Network Engineer
Whatzupnet – Jersey City, NJ

- Second-level Network support was provided for a worldwide network with over 4,000 nodes.
- Configured, upgraded, and performed troubleshooting for multiple network devices and router systems, and switch platforms and Cisco Catalyst 6500 chassis network switches.
- Implemented network changes and verified functionality and firewall ability.
- Provisioned, maintained, and troubleshot Nortel passport network, serving as Instinet's global private ATM network.
- Created and maintained HO OpenView Map for WAN with 4,000+ nodes.
- Applied functional knowledge of HP UNIX, Sun Solaris, and Windows Operating Systems to troubleshoot server network problems.

Highlights:

+ Upgraded routers and switches to the latest codes to work around computer issues associated with Y2K.
+ Worked 48 hours to replace data center lost in the World Trade Center North Tower, building out infrastructure in the New Jersey Data Center to accommodate the additional load.

EDUCATION

Control Data Institute of Technology
A.S. Computer Science

Staten Island Community College
A.A.S. Programming

JOSH PRANESH

Austin, TX | 979-255-8438 | praneshrj@gmail.com

Senior Software Engineer

Software professional with in-depth experience developing both infrastructure and products. Strong understanding of computer architecture, programming languages and system design principles. Proven ability to ensure quality and predictability for software development. Excellent communication skills and proven ability to work with customers, engineers, and business stakeholders. Keen interest in learning and in the application of machine learning techniques to real-world problems.

Highlights

> Infrastructure Development and Automation, Configuration Management, Distributed System Design.
> Requirements/Feature Definition, Business & User Requirements, Software Product Development and Releases, Software Quality, Software Development Life Cycle.
> Recruiting and Team Development, Technical Leadership, Engineering Project Management
> Machine Learning/AI.

Technology Summary

- C/C++, C#, Python, & Scripting (Powershell, Bash, Batch)
- Windows, Linux, & Mac OS X
- Visual Studio, Git, Perforce, Azure DevOps, PyCharm, GNU Make, Google Test, xUnit.
- SaltStack, Packer (by HashiCorp), SCVMM (by Microsoft).

Professional Experience

Senior Software Engineer   May 2017 – Present
IBM - Austin - TX
Delivered several infrastructure improvement projects while continuing to work on NI's installer architecture. Continued participating in recruiting effort.
Key Accomplishments:
- Infrastructure as Code - Automated the process of deploying and setting up VMs used as installer build machines for LabVIEW NXG and its add-ons.
- Service Account Password Management - Developed a system and work-flows to manage service account passwords that are used to access machines building production bits.
- Package Validation Utility - Owned and added many rules to validate packages and feeds during the internal build process.
- LabVIEW NXG and Addons installers - Designed packages and feeds for built binaries.
- Package Manager - Support for installation analytics.
- Recruiting - On-site interviews and on-campus at Texas A&M University, College Station.

JOSH PRANESH – Page 2
555-250-8439 | praneshjjt@gmail.com

Staff Software Engineer   *July 2011 - May 2017*
IBM - Austin - TX
Developed multiple iterations of NI's installer architecture while continuing to work on NI's licensing architecture. Participated in recruiting effort.

Key Accomplishments:
- Improved build process to better integrate localized error strings into Package Manager.
- Provided a notification system in the licensing architecture for volume license administrators.
- Designed an automated way to send licensing logs to NI to allow better support.
- Created installer packages for commonly used tools (like C++ runtimes and .NET framework).
- Recruiting - Conducted phone and on-site interviews.

Software Engineer   *September 2006 - July 2011*
IBM - Austin - TX
Developed multiple iterations of NI's licensing architecture - NI License Manager (NILM) and NI Volume License Manager (NI VLM).

Key Accomplishments:
- Improved product start-up and license activation experience.
- Designed NI VLM Engine to modularize VLM so that .NET UI could be developed on top of it.
- Designed user interface for settings and landing page of NI VLM.
- Re-designed NILM build process.

Education

Master of Science - Computer Science

Texas State University, College Station - TX

Bachelor of Science - Computer Science and Engineering
National Institute of Technology, Mumbai - India

KEVIN CHOY

Dallas, TX |555-321-1772 | kschoy999@gmail.com

SENIOR SOFTWARE DEVELOPER/ENGINEER

Highly motivated software development professional seeking to innovate, learn, and grow in an agile collaborative team environment. Solid understanding of design patterns, data structures, testing, and best practices. Expertise in DevOps methodologies and tools. Write clean, well-tested code. Independently design and build technical solutions. Use data structures and algorithms to solve problems. Design efficient, maintainable, and scalable features.

HIGHLIGHTS

Software Development Life Cycle	Code Review	Design Patterns
Relational/Transactional Databases	Testable Code	Design Structures
Use Cases	Continuous Integration	Containers/AWS
Backend/Frontend Development	Queries/Data Analysis	Transactional Systems

TECHNICAL SKILLS

Java • C++ • C# • HTML • CSS • JavaScript • MySQL • MongoDB • Spring MVC • Spring Boot • .NET Core • React

EDUCATION

Bachelor of Science in Engineering – Computer Science – University of Massachusetts

PROFESSIONAL EXPERIENCE

SENIOR SOFTWARE DEVELOPER   Aug 2018 – Dec 2021
HIGHPOINT LABS – **Braintree, MA**

- Assisted in research and fact-finding to develop and modify applications.
- Design and build technical solutions applying coding patterns and writing high-performing, testable code.
- Solve problems with algorithms and data structures.

Accomplishments:
- Shortened time and complexity of reconciliation process for Brazilian Period Average Cost calculations for accountants.
  - > Created calculation workflow and automated it, generating report for verification, reducing need to perform calculation and improving accuracy and generated report in minutes instead of multiple days.

CONTRACT SOFTWARE ENGINEER   Mar 2018 – Jul 2018
THE HOME DEPOT – **Darian, CT**

- Performed backend development focusing on Soring Boot and Google Cloud Pub/Sub to move email templating services to Google Cloud Platform.

Accomplishments:
- Built a modern system for intaking and sending email messages, focusing on testability.

SOFTWARE ENGINEER   Jun 2013 – Jun 2017
INDEED, INC. – **New York, NY**

- Added flexibility and functionality for credit card intake process including support for Brazilian, Indian, and Southeastern markets, working primarily in Java Spring MVC backend.

Accomplishments:
- Increased payment reach for two large emerging markets by enabling payment in new currencies.
- Saved $100K annually by facilitating compliance with PCI requirements.

Angelo Jordan

Columbus, OH   ajor222@gmail.com   740-555-9091

Systems Analyst

A versatile member of the IT project team performing the roles of requirements specialist, test leader, and project manager. Successfully build relationships to learn requirements, understand business processes, document use cases, and translate business requirements into systems solutions. Develop solutions addressing a wide range of problems, applying technical knowledge, concepts, and theories in recommending the best systems approach.

Core Competencies

Business Processes | Business Use Cases | Systems Integration- | Data Mapping
System Enhancements | Stakeholder Business Requirements | New System Implementation
System Enhancements | User Acceptance Testing (UAT) | Control Documentation
Technical Standards | Application Lifecycle Support | New Application Design/Development

PROFESSIONAL EXPERIENCE

Geico Insurance – Columbus, OH | Jul 2009 - Current
SPECIALIST/SYSTEMS ANALYSIS

Application Enhancement Coordination Lead for a suite of claims handling systems, scoped enhancements, and defect fixes for monthly application releases. Coordinate team of developers in design and coding to meet test readiness and release milestones.

- Application Enhancement Coordination Lead for a suite of claims handling systems; scoped enhancements and defect fixes for monthly application releases. Coordinated team of developers in design and coding to meet test readiness and release milestones.

- Eliminated defect backlog by classifying, prioritizing, and resolving 200+ production defects by recommending solution approaches, gathering and documenting business requirements, and formulating test plans.

- Trained team members and served as SME for Enterprise Defect Standardization project and coached analysts and developers in new standard implementation within the Quality Center defect tracking tool.

- Developed master test strategy as Project Test Lead for document management system implementation, defined UAT strategy, and conducted UAT via an end-user forum framework.

- Remedied and re-launched initial failed release of Claims Transformation (CT) Program Pilot by re-designing the activation plan for rollout of new Guidewire packaged software.

- Requirements Lead for CT Program Release 2, developing system requirements and data mappings for agile Integration Team, to convert vendors' electronic data feeds to the new Guidewire software platform.

- Feature Owner for CT Program Release 3, building solid partnerships with external vendors' IT and operations leadership teams; developed work breakdown structure and led Iteration Planning for over 100 stories to build and activate Worker's Comp medical bill management and regulatory compliance reporting.

- Presented recommendations to CT program and business leadership for multi-company integrations for pilot activation of Guidewire Software, enabling regional rollouts of the new system.

ANGELO JORDANI | Page 2 ✉ ajor222@gmail.com ☎ 740-555-9091

⚑ Walter B. Cooke – New York, NY | May 2006 - Jun 2009
SYSTEMS SOLUTIONS CONSULTANT

- Managed IT capital budget for project portfolio mix at AEP, and developed customer requirements into project proposals, presenting business cases for funding approval.
- Produced systems requirements documents and held usability forums with end-users.
- Implemented Kronos timekeeping system in manufacturing plants throughout the U.S.
- Documented system configuration requirements based on pay practices and contractual compliance needs.
- Coordinated parallel testing exercises and production rollouts for each Grief Services, Inc. plant.
- Consultant for onsite fieldwork for audits of government entities and school districts.

⚑ Universal Brands, Inc. – Dayton, OH | Sept 1999 – Mar 2006
MANAGER – IT OPERATIONS SUPPORT

Oversaw development and ongoing support for enterprise supply chain/logistics management system. Created strategic annual plans for system functionality enhancements and presented business cases for funding, including front-end web applications and backend/database upgrades.

- Led multiple systems project through the project development lifecycle, including requirements definition, functional design, technical specifications, testing, training, and implementation.
- Integrated inbound logistics services and customer compliance functions into single systems network for sister company.
- Improved supply chain operating processes by implementing a series of electronic information flows (EDI transactions) from logistics trading partners, leveraging in-transit visibility to build exception-based inventory tracking.

--- EDUCATION & CERTIFICATIONS ---

Master of Professional Accountancy
Old Dominion University

Bachelor of Business Administration
West Carolina College

FRANK AMORE

Email: amore_frank@yahoo.com

Maintenance Manager

Seasoned, experienced maintenance engineer with 25+ years of experience playing a vital role in commercial and residential building capital programs and maintenance. Highly skilled in facility management, organization, supervision, communication, and team work. Lead, train, and develop high performing teams to meet project deadlines on time and under budget. Strong customer service and problem-solving skills. Complete understanding applicable building and fire codes, OSHA regulations and applicable housing regulations.

Skills

Project Management | Operations Management | Operations Management | Contract Negotiation
Vendor Management | Inventory Control / Management | Mechanical / HVAC / Plumbing Systems
Attention to Detail | Landscaping / Irrigation / Septic Systems | Budget Management / Cost Control
Swimming Pool Certification | Team Supervision and Training | Blueprint Reading

Professional Experience

Maintenance Engineer   3/2017 – 3/2021
Kenwood Inn and Spa, Kenwood, CA

- Managed multiple capital projects and maintenance programs for Sonoma Wine Country Mediterranean-style inn located on 2.5 acres, meticulously landscaped with greenery, flowers, courtyard, and pool facility.
- Planned, scoped, scheduled, and executed upgrading and remodeling projects for building interiors and exteriors and landscaping.
- Reduced maintenance and repair costs by 25% by implementing a preventive maintenance program.
- Implemented new safety program with no recordable OSHA incidents during tenure.
- Sourced new contractors to improve on-time response and save money.
- Conducted regular inspections and implemented routine preventive maintenance, ensuring optimal performance of water heaters, electrical panels, water, septic and well pumps, and HVAC.

Maintenance Supervisor   8/2009 – 3/2017
Bitter Creek LLC, Osborne, CA

- Directed 11-member team in managing a diverse portfolio of properties that included a winery, office buildings, warehouse, apartment building, wine tasting bar and restaurant.
- Planned major building renovations and upgrades by inspecting properties, developing budgets and estimates, and bidding specialty work to contractors.
- Implemented processes for preventive maintenance inspections and repair.
- Monitored the quality of work performed by contractors and staff.
- Maintained project schedules, budgets, and expense records.
- Worked on historic preservation class properties and obtained special work permits.
- Implemented safety program with no major injuries or safety incidents for seven years.

Education & Training

- **High School Diploma -** Mi Casa Grande High School, Petaluma, WA
- OSHA Construction Safety Training

L Y N N E T T E   F R O M M E ,   R N

Boise, ID | 888-330-3333 | lfromme123g@yahoo.com

REGISTERED NURSE

A skilled, compassionate and accomplished registered nurse with more than 20 years of experience as an Emergency Room and Charge Nurse. Implement and develop the plan of care, maintaining medical reports and assessing patient's requirements. Possess good communication and management skills. Experience in intensive care, acute medical and emergency room care. In-depth knowledge of nursing supervision and professional development. Good communication and interpersonal skills. Goal oriented and excellent team player, possessing good monitoring and supervisory skills and attention to detail.

CORE COMPETENCIES

Emergency Care	Plan of Care	Supervisory Guidance
Triage	Patient Assessment /Evaluation	Nursing Best Practices
Training & Mentoring	Health Education	Standards of Care
Staff Development	Pediatric / Geriatric Care	Quality Improvement
Charge Nurse	Pre-Post-Op Care	Cultural Sensitivity
Patient Data Collection	JCHAO Compliance	Documentation

PROFESSIONAL EXPERIENCE

DEPARTMENT OF VETERANS AFFAIRS | Boise, ID   2008 – 2020
REGISTERED NURSE – EMERGENCY CARE | CHARGE NURSE

- Deliver comprehensive, high quality, cost effective healthcare to Veteran patients.
- Maintain certification in BLS, ACLS, and PALS.
- Provide age-based care to meet the physical, mental, and emotional needs of patients.
- Document observations, assessments, and changes in patient condition.
- Collaborate with interdisciplinary team members to achieve positive patient care outcomes.
- Demonstrate effective communication skills with patients, families, visitors, and team members.
- Administer a variety of treatment modalities, including oxygen, immunizations, IV fluid, blood transfusions, and prescribe oral, subcutaneous, and intramuscular medications.
- Lead practitioners and support teams as charge nurse in delivering primary care, case management, and medication management.
- Experience in the Clinical Procedures Center in the Cath Lab and floater to EP lab, IR, and Clinical Procedures Center for pre-and post-op assistance.

WEST NILE COMMUNITY HOSPITAL | West Nile, CA   2007 - 2009
STAFF AND CHARGE NURSE – EMERGENCY ROOM

- Worked within a team of healthcare professionals to provide care, monitor health conditions, plan long term care needs, administer medicine, use medical equipment, and perform medical procedures.
- Quickly assessed needs of each patient and prioritize care based on clinical assessments and evaluation.
- Compassionately interacted with people in various states of pain, trauma, and tragedy.
- Guided less experienced nurse, made assignments, and fielded complaints from patients.
- Maintained calm and assertive during high pressure situations.

WOLVERINE PRESBYTERIAN MEDICAL CENTER | Wolf's Edge, ME　　　2005 - 2006
REGISTERED NURSE – EMERGENCY ROOM

- Worked cooperatively with physicians, nurses, and technicians for long established acute care facility serving local multicultural communities.
- Assumed responsibility for coordinating safe, efficient, and therapeutically effective age-specific nursing care.
- Supported patient safety initiatives and quality improvement activities.
- Collected and assessed patient data and interpreted data appropriately to identify patient needs.

MAGA HEALTHCARE | Warm Springs, GA　　　2002 - 2007
TRAVEL NURSE

- Assigned to hospitals on a per-diem basis throughout Phoenix, AZ and Los Angeles, CA.
- Performed initial patient assessments, measured and recorded vital statistics and medical histories, and evaluated patients' psychological, emotional, and physical well-being; order and interpret diagnostic tests and labs.
- Worked with interdisciplinary healthcare team to formulate, implement, and modify individual plans of care, including discharge instructions.
- Observed and reported abnormal vital sign changes and symptoms to physicians to determine next course of action.
- Demonstrated strong clinical skills in venipuncture, IV therapy, medication administration, wound care, and ventilator management.
- Educated patients and caregivers on disease process, diagnosis, treatment options, and expected outcomes.
- Informed patients on self-administration of medication, disease self-management, and lifestyle management to sustain recovery process after hospital discharge.
- Provided professional comfort and emotional support to patients, families, and caregivers to reduce anxiety and provided counsel and relief from fear, anger or grief.

EDUCATION

Bachelor of Science in Nursing, Chandler University, Chandler, AZ
Associate Degree in Nursing, Desert Palm Community College, Phoenix, AZ

LICENSURE AND CERTIFICATION

Registered Nurse, ID, ME, NY, CA
IV and ACLS Certified

CYNTHIA BLACK

Las Vegas, NV | 702-111-2345 | CindyB222@gmail.com

OFFICE MANAGER

"Go to" problem solver with a can do attitude. Able to meet the demands of the organization in a fast paced environment. Trusted advisor to senior management. Good business acumen, decision making, and judgment. Customer focused, developing good client relationships. Very flexible with demonstrated ability to support office operations, sales and marketing, accounting, and account management functions. Positive, upbeat, and self-starting, well organized, with attention to detail. Tech-savvy with excellent written and verbal communication skills.

KEY SKILLS

Bookkeeping • Project Management • Office Administration • Accounts Payable / Receivable
Collections • Customer Relationships • Collections • Ethics & Confidentiality • Customer Service •Import / Export
Meetings •Travel Itinerary • Phone System Management • Presentations
Warehouse Management • Call Screening / Reception • Shipping & Receiving
Client Account Management • Calendar Management   Complex Reports • Communications   Regulatory Compliance •
Sound Judgment • Decision Making • File Management • Spreadsheets

WORK HISTORY

Nifty Fashions, Las Vegas, NV   2014 - Present
Office Manager/Account Manager
- Authorized wholesale representative for 11 retro-clothing retail lines for clients based in the U.S. and Europe.
- Represent companies by traveling internationally as well as domestically to trade shows.
- Organize trade show presentations, including orders, shipping, set-up, and merchandising.
- Launch marketing and sales campaigns through networking and the use of social media.
- Grew business from under $50,000 to $2.5 million in annual sales over five years.

BETTY BOOK CLOTHING / LOS ALAMOS, CA   2008-2014
Executive Assistant / Wholesale Operations Manager
- Worked in a client-facing capacity assisting senior management in sales and order fulfillment.
- Screened, checked and prioritized emails and correspondence from domestic and international customers.
- Managed company events and trade shows, planning international travel itinerary.
- Tracked and managed inventory for 20 retail stores operated by the company, and managed website sales, and coordinated retail and wholesale business operations.
- Managed the order and payment cycle for business transactions, using QuickBooks to track sales and revenue.
- Placed orders with manufacturers and the warehouse, monitored delivery times, and worked with customs broker for Import arrival of shipments.
- Revamped warehouse operations by implementing a new warehouse inventory tracking system reducing missing or unaccounted inventory and improving on-time delivery.
- Created concept of recycling excess inventory from retail stores for the next selling season.
- Generated revenue by introducing sales promotions for wholesale and retail operations.

CYNTHIA BLACK | 702-111-2345 | CindyB222@gmail.com

ACQ LANDSCAPE DESIGN + CONSTRUCTION, Henderson, NV 2006 – 2007
Office Manager / Bookkeeper
- Represented the company to customers while creating and maintaining relationships within the company and externally with vendors, suppliers, and other parties.
- Full charge administrative manager, including accounting, billing, collections, and bookkeeping operations.
- Managed A/R, A/P, quarterly taxes, payroll, customer tracking, scheduling client services and appointments, allowing owner to focus on sales and productivity.
- Proactively communicated with customers, employees, sub-contractors, and vendors, tech-savvy and comfortable working in a fast-paced environment.

HOLY GRAIL HUMANITARIAN FOUNDATION, Los Angeles, CA 2001 – 2003
Director of Development & Special Events
- Prepared annual development plan, revenue budget, and calendar of events.
- Provided monthly reports for financial donations and expenses.
- Organized and implemented celebrity golf tournaments, auctions, speaker tours, and banquet dinners.
- Launched successful fundraising campaigns and developed granting foundation relationships.
- Built relationships in the community to raise awareness of the program for the east/west coast operations.

JUDEA COMMUNITY CENTERS OF GREATER NAPA VALLEY, Grapevine, CA 1996 – 2001
Office Manager
- Received and screened walk-in visitors, addressed needs, and directed to appropriate department.
- Screened and directed calls and processed mail, directing to appropriate parties.
- Maintained inventory levels for office supplies.
- Performed word processing, maintained file systems, and implemented efficient operations.
- Assigned to special projects as required, working in a self-directed manner to meet deadlines.
- Delivered successful fundraising events including auctions, banquets, and dances.
- Screened and reviewed applications for scholarships and made award recommendations.
- Managed tuition payments and reconciled accounts through quarterly, monthly, and weekly reviews.
- Coordinated multiple tasks and projects efficiently for office operations, the preschool program, and childcare center.

EDUCATION

Diploma, Edward R. Monroe High School, Walden, NY

SKILLS

MS Office Suite (Excel, Word, Outlook), QuickBooks
Social Media Platforms, Internet

MATTHEW GATES

Phoenix, AZ • 555-181-0285 • matthewg@yahoo.com • www.linkedin.com/in/mattyg-b144433/

OPERATIONS MANAGEMENT
Logistics • Security • Capital Projects

Dynamic Security and Logistics management professional with proven leadership under challenging conditions, skilled in security patrols and missions. Driven to overcome challenges to meet goals, leveraging the ability to lead and collaborate, applying substantial knowledge of supply chains and logistics. Committed to optimizing and coordinating processes. Advanced training and experience in weapons, law enforcement, and crowd control. Exceptional ability to prioritize multiple daily tasks to ensure work is completed with minimal supervision.

HIGHLIGHTS

Operations Management • Patrol/Military Base Security • Inventory Management
Project Management • Secret Clearance Eligible • Asset Management • Supply Chain Management
Performance Management • Process Improvement • Tactual Situation Management
Supplier Negotiation • Budget/Cost Control • Purchasing/Procurement • Detention/Interrogation
Warehouse Management • Commercial Logistics • Team Leadership/Supervision
Customer Relations • Training & Development • Personnel Management

KEY QUALIFICATIONS

▸ Proven business leader managing projects in an agile, fast-paced, deadline driven environment, applying critical solutions, and improving current practices.
▸ Execute mission operations, surveillance, logistics coordination, inventory management, and security management.
▸ Expertise in force and personal protection, crowd control, law enforcement, security patrols, commanding subordinates, providing direction, mainlining weapons, and equipment, and coordinating programs.
▸ Skilled in Land Navigation Methods, Map & Compass, GPS, and Biometrics Automated Toolset (BAT) System.
▸ Protection of high-ranking political figures and military officers from the Iraqi Government and branches of the US military.
▸ Implement improvements in utilizing space, managing inspection, shipping, handling, and distributing supplies.

PROFESSIONAL EXPERIENCE

KKK ENERGY SOLUTIONS – New Orleans, LA   **Sep 2019 – Current**
OPERATIONS MANAGER
- Developed business plan for launch of commercial management, risk-mitigation advisory, and dispute resolution services for complex projects across the construction and engineering space.
- Coordinated and negotiated terms with subcontractors, vendors, and suppliers.
- Developed key performance indicators and identified performance deficiencies and required corrective actions.
- Collaborated with customer business units to develop integrated digital strategies.
- Identified business requirements to recommend IT development plans and implement change management.

ALVARO ESPERANZA

Atlantic City, NJ | alelsp@gmail.com | (555) 123-1320

AREA / REGIONAL SALES MANAGER

Outside Sales Professional with proven record of profit and revenue growth in assigned territories through strategic planning execution, customer engagement, and follow-up. Passion for sales, management of existing relationships, and development of new partnerships. Drive sales plans and forecasting. Gain new distribution and promotional activity through direct intervention with sales teams and customers. Provide exceptional customer service by understanding customer needs and providing product and service solutions. Proactively partner within the organization to introduce new products to market. Analyze data to understand market trends and competitor activity in the region.

HIGHLIGHTS

Territory Growth Management | Inbound & Outbound Prospecting | Sales Life Cycle Management
Competitor & Market Analysis | Food Service/Retail/Grocery | Sales Pipeline Management
Product Value Proposition | Account Penetration | Performance Management/KPIs
Sales Presentations | Sales Closing Ability | Product & Service Solutions
Business Communications | Product Introduction | Inventory Management | Profit & Loss
Strategic Customer Relations | Customer Service/Retention

PROFESSIONAL EXPERIENCE

CASTER OILS – Boston, MA   Sep 2018 – Jan 2020
Regional Area Sales Manager – Food Service

- Successfully planned, organized, and executed sales plans that gained new clients and increased penetration of existing accounts.
- Analyzed business trends to develop and implement category strategies for profit and volume growth, using data to inform category direction, new product development recommendations, marketing needs, pricing, and distribution strategies.
- Built rapport with decision-makers in customers' organization and maintained customer loyalty and retention by responding to customer needs and offering product and service solutions.
- Mentored and guided field representatives and brokers to meet goal expectations for territory growth.
- Assumed ownership for strategic deal-making for neighborhood penetration within the territory.
- Maintained deep knowledge of competitive activities and risks to market share and developed effective value proposition for product line including pricing strategies to counter efforts to penetrate accounts.

BURT'S EXOTIC CHEESE – Perth Amboy, NJ   Apr 2014 – Mar 2018
Regional Area Sales Manager – Food Service

- Exceeded quarterly sales goals in the New York Metro sales division by monitoring performance metrics and identifying opportunities for growth, generating almost $40M and 10M lbs. of product annually.
- Guided 14 member sales team in exceeding goals by 25% year over year, netting $2M in net sales.
- Resolved customer issues through active listening, communication, and advocacy to retain customers.
- Monitored performance by each route in the division and reviewed accounts receivable reports to drive increased business within existing accounts and development of new accounts in each route.

ALVARADO ESPERANZA – Page 2

alelsp@gmail.com | (555) 123-1320

THE BEVERAGE BOSS – Fairfield, NJ   Jun 2013 – Apr 2014
Account Manager
- Supported a team of Large Format Managers and Merchandisers in servicing national grocery and mass-merchandising chains.
- Ensured trade merchandising standards in all retail accounts, representing brand identity.
- Provided current promotions, displays, and marketing tools for use by customers to drive product sales.
- Ensured that products were available and distributed to customers, following structured delivery frequency.
- Documented, analyzed, and summarized PNE delivery and inventory tracking statistics.
- Trained account representatives and managers in executing company policies and practices.
- Ensured that product merchandising in the energy drink category achieved 100% display execution.

ORTIZ FOOD CONSULTANTS – Woodbridge, NJ   Sep 2007 – Jun 2013
Product Marketing Manager
- Oversaw marketing and distribution of product line at the storefront operational level.
- Studies market analytics to design an engaging marketing strategy including collateral   content development.
- Assessed performance to identify and execute opportunities for improvement in market penetration and sales.

SEVEN-UP – Jersey City, NJ   Jun 2008 – Feb 2012
Commercial Sales Representative
- Led by example by driving sales and performance by identifying commercial prospects, scheduling appointments, presenting in-person sales proposals, and closing sales in assigned territory.
- Assisted customers in resolving billing and installation issues.
- Achieved Nationwide Sales Top Five ranking for three consecutive years.
- Consistently won quarterly Sales Achievement Circle Awards.

EDUCATION

Bachelor of Arts – Graphic Design Concentration
William Shatner University – Wayne, NJ

LANGUAGES

Bilingual – English and Spanish

TECHNOLOGY SKILLS

MS Office: Word, Excel, PowerPoint, Outlook, Adobe Creative Suite

RECENT GRADUATE'S RESUME

LISA STARK

Palo Alto, CA 91730 • (999) 555-3732 • |lstark111@gmail.com

ENTRY LEVEL PROJECT ENGINEER

Dedicated and hard-working college senior expecting a degree in Construction Management from Indiana State University in 2021. Education and experience in managerial and technical skills. Understand the impact of construction on the environment and the qualities of construction project leadership. Focused on creative and analytical problem-solving, working independently and as a collaborative member of the team. Capacity to function well in a fast-paced environment. Strong computer and office management skills. Academic studies include:

- ▶ Building design and planning.
- ▶ Environmental control systems.
- ▶ Principles of quality concrete and the proper techniques used in the field.
- ▶ Project management, including construction costs, budgets, bids, critical path scheduling, inspection, labor utilization, and cost control.
- ▶ Use of tapes, levels, and transits to layout structures, determine elevations, and locate boundaries.

HIGHLIGHTS

Architectural Drawing • Construction Management • Estimating/Cost Analysis • Soil Analysis
Computer Applications • Construction Scheduling • Electrical Construction • Supervision
Construction Inspection/Quality • Building Code Compliance • Mechanical Systems　Construction
Methods/Materials • Specifications/Contract Documents • Supervision　• Inspection

EDUCATION & CERTIFICATIONS

Bachelor of Science in Construction Management – Indiana State University – Terre Haute, Indiana 2020
Associate of Science in Business Administration – (Honors) Chaffey College – Rancho Cucamonga, CA **Associate of Science in Professional Office Management** – Chaffey College – Rancho Cucamonga, CA **Construction Management Certificates**, California State Polytechnic University, Pomona, CA
Construction Management • Project Engineering for Construction Management • Deciphering Construction Plans

WORK EXPERIENCE

KROGER'S　Dec 2015 – Aug 2020
OFFICE COORDINATOR

- Managed front-end operation of busy market with responsibility for balancing cash draws for sales.
- Created a culture at customer checkout for delivery of world-class customer care.
- Participated in hiring, training, and coaching department employees and ensuring compliance with SOPs.
- Assisted customers, resolved problems, and maintained security surveillance equipment.
- Anticipated staff coverage requirements and upheld customer service standards.

AMERICAN TAX SERVICES　Jan 2012 – Jan 2014
TAX PROFESSIONAL/FINANCIAL ADVISOR

- Assessed the financial status of clients to develop the best tax strategies and to take advantage of deductions, generally saving clients hundreds of dollars in overpayments to the IRS.
- Advised clients how to increase the earning power of their investments based on risk tolerance.

Recent Graduate's Resume

James Spinner

516-222-4203 • Jspiner123 @gmail.com

Media & Communications

Motivated, dedicated professional taking pride in working efficiently, collaboratively, and expeditiously. Team player thriving in an energetic, pressured environment, assisting. and supporting associates. Effective in communicating to targeted audiences. Think critically and creatively in developing research topics using appropriate resources and methods. Understand multiple perspectives, engaging productively by interpretation, analysis, argumentation, and reflection.

———— Highlights ————

- Writing/News Writing
- Document Layout
- Investigative Techniques
- Initiative/Self-Motivation

- Public Speaking
- Interviewing
- Targeted Audiences
- Teamwork

- Editing & Proofreading
- Public Speaking
- Active Listening Skills
- Compelling Copy

———— Education ————

Bachelor of Arts- Media and Communications – May 2020
Old Dominion University

- ▯ Course of Study: Critical Creative Thinking, Diversity, Knowledge of American Society, Media Studies, Journalism & Media, Writing for Media, Investigative Reporting, Media Production

Associate of Arts - Liberal Arts
Nassau County Community College – Garden City, NY

———— Professional Experience ————

THE CATALYST NEWSPAPER – OLD DOMINION UNIVERSITY   **Jan 2019 – May 2020**

PUBLISHER AND EDITOR
The Catalyst Newspaper and website serve as the student body's voice while providing valuable experience in covering the news, writing reviews, offering opinions, and discussing issues on and off-campus.
- Managed news staff and organized news stories for print issues.
- Took responsibility for all facets of the newspaper, made final editorial decisions, and stood by content produced.
- Chaired editorial meetings, supervised quality control, and controlled coverage.
- Gathered and verified information through interviews, observation, and research.
- Wrote columns, editorials, and commentary, and organized news stories for publication
- Discussed issues with editors to identify priorities, develop or revise policies and positions.
- Consistently met publication deadlines, handling a steady, heavy workload resulting in a smooth publication process for the team.
- Improved the quality of the paper by managing and mentoring writers and editorial staff.

———— Technology ————

MS Office Suite (Word, Excel, PowerPoint, Outlook • Adobe Acrobat • Adobe Premier

JOHN F. BOLTON

Bolton.john@gmail.com | 804-333-3332 | www.linkedin.com/in/john-f-bolton-615b2825

SALES DIRECTOR/BUSINESS OPERATIONS
Executive Sales Leader • Business Strategist Global • Technology Program Manager

Proven leader, hiring, mentoring, and developing high-performing sales teams to drive sales strategies, services, and delivery that provide value customers and increase market footprint. Strategically plan and implement winning sales strategies. Manage enterprise software application, channel management, and partner development. Align sales processes to business requirements. Ability to communicate, present, and influence all levels of the organization including executive and C-level.

HIGHLIGHTS

Sales Leadership • Sales Territory Development • Partner Development • Collaborative Solutions
Account Acquisition • Channel Management • Professional/Technical Support • Life Cycle Services
Cross-Functional Team Leadership • Sales Process Management • Emerging Market Trends
Solution Selling • Product Positioning • Resource Optimization • Go-to-Market Strategy
Emerging Technologies • Business Cases/Proposals/Pre-Sales • Negotiating/Influencing
Cloud Strategy/Migration • SaaS

PROFESSIONAL EXPERIENCE

Global Business Development Leader/Custom Enterprise Solutions   2015 - Present
WANG LABORATORIES

- Develop customized solutions favorably impacting on customer outcomes by leading global services business development team in providing unique solutions and gaining high customer satisfaction.
- Create sales capacity by understanding emerging technologies, market trends, and driving innovation.

Highlights:

- Consistently met and exceeded targets and performance metrics from 2015 to 2019 consecutively.
- Oversaw GIS-based SaaS application development that is revolutionizing delivery strategy and capabilities while containing costs.

Northeast Area Sales Manager – Enterprise Sales   2008 – 2014
WANG LABORATORIES

- Achieved services subscription revenue growth by leading Enterprise East team of service and consulting sellers.
- Increased Cisco revenue by building collaborative, cross-functional teams transforming customer businesses.
- Empowered team to achieve targets through mentoring, support, and service optimization.
- Evangelized importance of customer and partner satisfaction, motivating teams meet and exceed expectations.

North East Area Sales Manager - Continued

Highlights:

- Provided high-value business growth by partnering with Services, Product, Channel Partner and Capital counterparts, identified opportunities to increase sales capacity, and exceeded sales targets each year/
- Recipient of FY 2015 Manager Excellence Award.

Client Services Executive – Mid Atlantic   2000 - 2007
WANG LABORATORIES

- Accountable for service sales and renewals for Enterprise, Commercial and SLED regions.
- Advocated change of sales model that elevated customer experience.
- Built client relationships up to the C-level to effectively bring change and transform the organization.

Highlights:

- Gained recognition as trusted advisor and SME by channel partners, account teams, peers, and clients.
- Exceeded goals at 110% of plan year over year by leveraging relationships, internal Cisco resources, and key Cisco partners, driving go-to-market strategy and customer satisfaction.

National Sales Manager – Chicago   1999 - 2000
IBM

- Developed national sales plan and strategic execution across direct sales and distribution channels.
- Managed relationships with large U.S.-based printers and paper distributors.

Highlights:

- Exceeded sales targets and performance metrics for customer satisfaction.

National Sales Manager – Chicago   1999 - 2000
IBM

- Developed national sales plan and strategic execution across direct sales and distribution channels.
- Managed relationships with large U.S.-based printers and paper distributors.

Highlights:

- Exceeded sales targets through direct sales and distribution channels.

EDUCATION

Master of Business Administration
Washington State University – Seattle, WA

Executive Leadership Program
Harvard School of Business

Bachelor of Arts
College of William and Mary

CERTIFICATION

ITIL Certified
Cisco Customer Experience Certified

DALLAS F. JACKSON, JR.

Hitching Post, NC 27521 | 919-999-2469 - |DFJ@me.com | https://www.linkedin.com/in/dallas-3970466/

SENIOR SALES ENGINEER

Technical expert and organizational leader focused on customer business solutions. Collaborate with account executives, customer experience managers, inside sales, and marketing to support technical justifications and business consultations during the customer's journey. More than 20 years of experience working with multi-million dollar accounts. Ensure compelling demos and presentations to company prospects. Expertise in setting up environments, loading and using applications, creating databases, loading ETL, and supporting sales team initiatives.

- ➲ Recognized for understanding, anticipating, and meeting customer needs, applying a bias for action.
- ➲ Passion for winning and achieving business success, differentiating products, and services from the competition.
- ➲ Understand the business environment and external markets.
- ➲ Collaborate cross-functionally to drive a performance culture and the free flow of information and ideas to deliver requirements and enhancements for the customer.

CORE SKILLS

Presentations/Demonstrations | Technical Leadership | Use Cases/Demo Solutions Training/Mentoring
Customer Requirements | Product Features/Roadmaps | Security Systems
Technical Pre-Sales Engineering | Security Solutions Architecture | Service-Oriented Architecture
Development Best Practices | Code Infrastructure | Content Management Systems
Enterprise Software Systems | Technical Product Collateral | Account Strategy | Strategic Planning
Enterprise Web Applications | Go-to-Market Strategy

TECHNOLOGY

Application Installations/Usage:	MicroStrategy, SAP/Crystal Reports, Pendo.io, Celebrus, Teradata CRM, IMM, VCX, Teradata Vantage Analyst, Teradata Database and Client Utilities
Ancient Programming Languages:	Cobol, Fortran, Pascal
Current Programming Languages:	Delphi (Object Pascal, C, C++, Java, PHP, JavaScript, Basic Code/JSON
Web Technologies:	HTML, CSS, Bootstrap 4, Apache, Tomcat, WebSphere
Environments:	VMWare: vSphere, Workstation, Player, VirtualBox AWS, Kubernetes, Docker
Databases:	Teradata v2r6 thru v17, MS SQL Server, Hadoop, AsterData, Oracle, IBM DB/2

PROFESSIONAL EXPERIENCE

DIGITAL X CORPORATION | Raleigh, NC
GLOBAL SALES SUPPORT ENGINEER | Jan 2007 – Oct 2020
Demos/ Presentations

- » Supported development of Global Road Show of VCX and Analyst Product and Technologies as part of Teradata Answers World Tour.
- » Produced Marketing video highlighting Churn Analysis using application screenshots with Adobe Stock images used in Teradata Analytics Universe Convention.
- » Collaborated to create storyboard for video used in Annual User's Conference.

GLOBAL SALES SUPPORT ENGINEER - Continued

Training & Development
- » Guided interns in developing and deploying mobile applications into iTunes/Google Play stores.
- » Helped Teradata University Network setup a Marketing training environment for college students.
- » Installed and configured required applications for Digital X's Training environment.

Key Accomplishments:
- » Supported the transition of Digital X support from a Windows environment by developing a new approach to provide a demo environment.
- » Adopted and included a new demo environment upon acquiring a new company (Aprimo), migrating hosted environment from Peak 10 to AWS, and enabling MS SQL Server access.
- » Created virtual services and maintained development and production Demo environment.
- » Built a version of Digital X's Demo environment that could run on a 'shoebox' computer, which was more powerful than a laptop but portable for customer pre-sales demos.
- » Modified existing Marketing Operations Dashboard with new features and bug fixes, using Teradata Covalent Framework.

PITNEY BOWES CORPORATION/DIGITAL X CORPORATION | Raleigh, NC
ENGINEER – CUSTOMER INSTALLATION AND PRE-SALES DEMO SUPPORT | Jan 2000 – Dec 2006
- » Supported sales engagements and the installation of an innovative, new version of CRM product for Mohegan Sun.
- » Improved requirements gathering/analysis processes of Sales Organizations, Marketing Department, and Professional Services.
- » Developed and updated demo scenarios, plans, roadmaps, and content updates.
- » Monitored business presentation results and made improvements for more effective demos and presentation delivery.
- » Identified third party packages from partners and drove their inclusion in product programs.
- » Worked on deployment plans for application demos and secured approval of various regions.
- » Contributed to Proofs of Concept and Pilots.

Key Accomplishments:
- » Provided solution for Teradata/Ceres Sales and Marketing team, enabling demonstration of CRM software to prospects.
- » Worked with Teradata developers to modify a version of Teradata Database that would run on Windows laptop, enabling creation of self-contained demo environment running from a modular hard drive inserted into laptop.
- » Solution was accepted and used for Sales, Training, and Proofs of Concept exercises.

EDUCATION & PROFESSIONAL DEVELOPMENT

Bachelor of Science in Mathematics – Wison University | Biie Creek, NC
Coursework: Teradata SQL, C, C++, IBM DB2 Advanced SQL, Hands-On Java Programming,
Teradata Advanced SQL, Teradata Physical Database Design

Linda Jacobson

Elmira, NY| 555-879-7500 | jacab@me.com | LinkedIn URL

Certified Elementary School Teacher (Grades K-6)

Dedicated elementary teacher eager to resume full-time teaching career (currently a substitute for the Elmira Free School District. Proven ability to consistently perform teaching functions. Passionate for education and commitment to optimizing the academic success of students and the school. .

Skills

Classroom Management	Special Needs Children	Curriculum Development
Cultural Sensitivity	Inclusion	Academic Assessment
Standardized Testing	IEP Development	Critical Thinking
Patience	Organization	Teamwork
Time Management	Technology Skills	Conflict Resolution

Experience

ELMIRA ELEMENTARY SCHOOL, Elmira, NY
Substitute Teacher (K-12), 9/16 to Present
Elementary Teacher (K-6), 9/12 to 6/15

Hired as a full-time teacher following student teaching practicum, instructing all academic subject areas with classes with up to 30 students.

Key Contributions:

- Recognized for the quality of classroom teaching, lesson plans, and instructional materials used in teaching language arts, mathematics, science, and social studies.
- Developed innovative approaches aligned with best practices for meeting district goals in technology integration across the curriculum, literacy and diversity areas.
- Taught general population students and individuals with learning challenges and special needs within a mainstreamed, inclusive classroom.
- Redirected students indicating behavior problems and lead in-service on innovative classroom management concepts.
- Served on school committees for curriculum development and textbook review.
- Launched anti-bullying campaign and counseled students subject to intimidation and bullying. .
- Became a "first-to-call" resource in current substitute teaching role, typically working four days per week.
- Requested by many full-time staff to take over their classrooms during absences.
- Primary

Caregiver, 6/10 to 6/16

Left the classroom to care for elderly parent diagnosed with stage IV cancer. Provided daily care, assisted with financial affairs, and coordinated treatment with medical professionals and hospice team.

Education & Credentials

Chandler University — Chandler, AZ - BA in Elementary Education
New York Teacher Certification, Grades K-6 (current)

DANA ANDREWS

Allen, TX 75002 | 212-333-1234 | dana_a@yahoo.com.com | www.linkedin.com/in/dana-a443322/

SUPPLY CHAIN / WAREHOUSE MANAGER

Natural ability to provide comprehensive reporting, visibility, and data-driven analytics to achieve improvements

Warehouse management professional with proven ability to lead, guide, and coach employees to meet production, quality, and safety goals. Recognized for developing in-house tools that streamline manual tasks and for leading Six Sigma Lean processes. Develop data-driven actionable improvement plans for overall business performance.

CORE EXPERTISE

Warehouse Management | Key Performance Indicators/KPIs | Shipping/Receiving | Leadership
Lean/Six Sigma | Project Management | Customized Reporting | Supply Chain Management Data Management
Data Analytics | Inventory Management | Continuous Process Improvement Operations Management | Logistics
Management | Distribution Center Fulfilment Efficiencies |

PROFESSIONAL EXPERIENCE

SUPPLY CHAIN PROJECT MANAGER ✦ Kmart |2019-2020
Mapped out end-to-end order flow processes with a goal of phasing out legacy systems and moving to a single-platform solution.

▸ **Key Accomplishments**
  - Identified root causes for inefficiencies in warehouse order fulfilment.
  - Made process improvement recommendations to meet elevated consumer demand during the holiday shopping season.

LOGISTICS SYSTEM ANALYST ✦ Rent-A-Wreck | 2015-2018
Deployed multiple technologies to enable new Supply Chain functionality, enabling $50 Million in Cost of Goods Sold (COGS) savings. Supported operations from configuration to deployment, including facility, inventory, and equipment preparation for warehouse and routing software implementation. Provided technical support to 500+ end-users.

▸ **Key Accomplishments**
  - Recouped $1.8 million in freight damages by eliminating a gap in support by the IT Department for freight claim tracking and submission.
  - Developed, coded, and deployed software tool permitting multiple users to create freight claims and track through resolution, and provided users with a Freight Claims user guide, with unique username and password.
  - Saved $100,000 by eliminating the need to retain third party testing software developer for the tracking of employee certifications for the WMS by creating a testing model to determine proficiency in Red Prairie, enabling users to receive a certificate of completion.

DANA ANDREWS – Page 2

212-333-1234 | dana_a@yahoo.com.com

USPS NATIONAL ACCOUNTS MANAGER ◆ Red-Box | 2012-2014

Ensured compliance with all active programs, updates, and pricing changes as company's national liaison with USPS. Provided special reports to senior management using Access, SQL, and Oracle applications. Managed weekly transportation freight bills and general ledger coding.

▸ **Key Accomplishments**

- Streamlined manual tasks and improved tracking and visibility by applying skills in database creation. Maintenance and manipulation.
- Ensured that USPS related expenses including administrative fees and Qualified Business Reply Mail were paid.

MANAGER, TRANSPORTATION ◆ Red-Box | 2010-2012

Team leader for daily transportation activities in a multi-channel network and maintained service levels above 98%. Analyzed data and provided senior management with actionable transportation metrics and data-driven recommendations for corrective actions to improve performance.

▸ **Key Accomplishments**

- Forecast an annual budget based on historical trends, unit projections, and seasonality.
- Developed year-in-review summary to provide roadmap for improvements in customer service and performed continuous improvement analysis of team activities.

TRAINING & SKILLS

Lean Six Sigma Black Belt | Warehouse Management System (WMS) Red Prairie | MS Access

JONATHAN SEAGAL

Fredericksburg, VA | 555-220-5632 | jonsea@gmail.com

DISTRIBUTION SPECIALIST

Dedicated material management professional focused on resolving and fulfilling customer requests professionally and timely. Organized, with attention to detail and excellent customer service skills. Familiar with inventory management, vendor and carrier relations, and supply chain synchronization. Use multiple software applications during performance of operations.

Core Skills

Receipt & Distribution Operations • Warehouse SOPS • Operations Management • Team Leadership
Customer Service • Transportation Management • Workflow Management • Process Improvements
Logistics Planning/Forecasting • Lean/Six Sigma Methodologies • Keyboarding/Computer Inputting

PROFESSIONAL EXPERIENCE

Amazon.com – Dupont, MI (Aug 2015 – Feb 2021)
Inbound Dock Clerk | Apr 2019 – Feb 2021

- Ensured continuous and steady flow of work to inbound vendor dock and inbound receiving dock, enabling receiving team to maintain productivity and reach daily vendor receive unit goals.
- Utilized web resources and Microsoft applications to identify optimal freight in the trailer yard.
- Strategically determined trailers that were optimal for each dock door and receiver ones allowed inbound receive department to safely cycle docks with new freight and enable earlier driver dispatch.
- Mastered Dockmaster, an Amazon search engine for inbound scheduling and yard and freight management tools.

Highlights:

- ▶ Reduced average appointment unload time from 72 hours to 24 hours for inbound vendor drops and three hours to one hour for Live load appointments by devising a new Excel Tool to manage workflow and trailer appointments.
- ▶ Achieved best productivity rates, averaging 95% for vendor goals, up from 79%, and attaining the highest average priority score of 98% up from 86% over two quarters, turning around productivity rates.

RSR Process Assistant | Jun 2020 – Aug 2020

- Supported department and daily management by leading meetings, allocating labor, communicating with internal and external suppliers, and covered for Area Managers.
- Trained associates and verified SOP compliance, ensuring successful area performance through tracking and reporting.
- Participated in safety initiatives and coached new employees on Amazon's culture of safety.

Highlights:

- ▶ Defined RSR Process Assistant role at site by developing an established standard of work and educated Process Assistants on operations and responsibilities.
- ▶ Achieved considerable drop in Defects per Million Opportunities (DPMO) benchmark and increased department productivity in all processes, exceeding established performance goals.
- ▶ Drove site from 5th in the network to 2nd in replenishment execution within two quarters of reorganization of RSR operations, improving ability to fulfill customer orders to meet demand.

JONATHAN SEAGAL | PAGE 2
555-220-5632 | jonsea@gmail.com

Outbound Shipping Clerk | Apr 2020 – Jun 2020
- Coordinated trailers to corresponding dock doors and cross docks using Outbound Manifest Accuracy tool to troubleshoot shipping problems and errors and communicate to other associates.
- Worked flexibly as Ship Dock Process Assistant and ship Clerk.

Highlights:
  ▸ Supervised shipping team in meeting daily performance goals, with a focus on quality and safety at the height of the COVID-19 pandemic, leading team to produce 4,000+ unit hours at 30+ throughput per hour (TPH) consistently.

Inbound Dock Process Guide | Apr 2018 – Apr 2020
- Ensured that each step of the process was completed and communicated accurately for item, quantity, unit of measurement, and other required information.
- Acted as an ambassador for new hires and served as resource for problem-solving,
- Managed floor and engaged associates with productivity and quality issues, ensuring compliance with strict safety, quality, and production standards.

Highlights:
  ▸ Created process map visual for Automatic Ground Vehicle operation for use across shifts.
  ▸ Maintained highest case replenishment rates placing second highest of four shifts.

Dock Worker | Aug 2015– Apr 2018
- Operated different types of warehouse equipment, including RC stand-up, double walkie, order picker, turret, and reach trucks.
- Performed inbound vendor pallet receiving and performed at the expected production rate.

EDUCATION

- **Associate of Arts – Liberal Arts**
  Huntington Community College – Huntington, NY

TECHNICAL SKILLS

- MS Office Suite, Word, Excel, PowerPoint, Dockmaster Search Engine, Yard Management Systems, Freight Management Consoles

---

CERTIFICATIONS

Forklift Operator Certification
OSHA 10 Hour Safety Training

Maria Romano

The Woodlands, TX 77381 | 200-236-4999 | mromano@outlook.com

MEDICAL LABORATORY TECHNICIAN

Quality-focused and collaborative certified medical lab technician returning to the laboratory after teaching elementary school subjects as a certified science and math teacher. Passionate about helping diagnose and prevent illnesses and diseases. Excellent clinical skills gained through hands-on experience in the U.S. Air Force.

Core Competencies

Regulatory Compliance | Recordkeeping/Documentation | Equipment Maintenance
Antigen Screens | Clinical Laboratory Procedures | Parasites/Disease | Urinalysis
Antibody Identification | Instrument Calibration | Inventory Control | Toxicology Screening
Sample/Reagent Preparation | Cell Counts | Metabolic & Electrolyte Panels

WORK EXPERIENCE

ELEMENTARY SCHOOL TEACHER   2009 – 2021

- Certified teacher, providing instruction to elementary school students in mathematics and science.
- Taught curriculum incorporating science experiments and elementary principles of biology, chemistry, and physics.
- Provided instruction to a broad range of diverse students of varying cultural and academic backgrounds.
- Increased passing rates for 5th grade students by taking a Science Coach position, initiating weekly Science in Review quizzes and intervention groups for low-performing students, with almost 100% passing grade for Science TAKS test.
- Worked with teachers to develop content and skill-building in the teaching of science to elementary students as school Science Coach.

MEDICAL LABORATORY TECHNICIAN – NORTHWEST MEDICAL CENTER   1993 – 2003

- Performed data entry and laboratory specimen processing.
- Organized and processed orders and provided excellent customer service.
- Checked working materials inventory and evaluated consumable levels to prevent shortages and expiration of supplies.
- Performed bench work including sample and reagent preparation.
- Operated and maintained laboratory equipment.
- Followed routine laboratory testing, following established standard operating procedures.

Maria Romano – Page 2

MILITARY EXPERIENCE

▌ **MEDICAL LAB TECHNICIAN, UNITED STATES AIR FORCE**
- ▸ Conducted analyses of tissue and body fluids for disease or abnormalities, checking body fluids for signs of disease and checking blood levels.
- ▸ Followed standard operating procedures for maintaining and cleaning the lab, calibrating, and maintaining laboratory equipment, including cell counters, microscopes, analyzers, incubators, and centrifuge machines.
- ▸ Assembled findings from tests on specimens into reports of laboratory findings.

Highlights:
- ● Managed front section of lab, including phlebotomies, shipping, urinalysis, serology testing, and reorganized sections to enable technicians to handle all sections while maintaining quality control and documentation easily.
- ● Recognized for control of specimens and elimination of backlog of reporting and documentation.
- ● Assisted in rewriting microbiology procedures for the laboratory with updates to current standards.
- ● Decreased workload caused by contamination by updating to an automated blood culture analysis process.
- ● Streamlined work processes in the microbiology section.

EDUCATION

BS in Interdisciplinary Studies
University of Alabama

Associate in Applied Science
Community College of the Air Force, Brooklyn, M

CERTIFICATIONS

Medical Laboratory Assistant Certification
ASCP Board of Certification - 2000

Texas Educator Certificates

Science 4-8 | Social Studies 4-8 | Generalist EC-6 | ESL/Generalist EC-6

ONE MORE THING!

- As before COVID-19, your resume plays a crucial role in the success or failure of your job search. It remains the primary method to gain an interview.
- The objective is simple: your resume needs to get you in the door.
- Write a resume that creates excitement by targeting resumes to specific formats. Don't use Word resume templates. They will confuse ATS scanning software.
- Use the hybrid resume format because it starts with the reason an employer should hire you, has all the keywords the employer is looking for, and has accomplishments that show your value.

8

APPENDIX

Articles by Al Palumbo, MBA, CPRW

- ➢ Is your resume a job description or a marketing tool that demonstrates your value?

- ➢ Advice about applicant tracking system software that companies use to select applicants for interviews.

- ➢ Are you a Do-er or an Achiever? What does your resume say you are?

- ➢ When it comes to resumes, don't put the cart before the horse. Target the job before you write!

- ➢ The art of the cover letter.

IS YOUR RESUME A JOB DESCRIPTION OR A MARKETING TOOL THAT DEMONSTRATES YOUR VALUE?

By Al Palumbo, MBA, CPRW
October 19, 2018

I see it all the time. Clients need resumes because their companies have downsized, gone offshore, or because they want to take advantage of the so-called full employment economy and make a change. I ask them to send me their most current resumes, and what I get are a series of job descriptions. I call this the "do-er" resume....I did this, I did that....and every single detail of their job functions are presented. It is not unusual to get a resume from a client with 10, 15 even 20 bullet points after each job.

Do you really think an employer needs to know every function and task that you perform on a job and do you think they are going to read this stuff? In my view the ideal resume needs two things....The first is the use of key words in your resume that reflect the hard and soft skills that employers are looking for and they often provide clues in their job descriptions.

But today I want to talk about the VALUE PROPOSITION of a resume. The heart of this is simple. Have you ever gone to job interview where the employer asks "WHY SHOULDI HIRE YOU"? There are variations of this question, some are subtler, but the bottom line is "WHAT CAN YOU BRING TO THE ORGANIZATION"? The best way to answer this, in your resume and in an interview is to demonstrate your value.

Yes, you need to put some description of a job function in the resume for context, but you can also describe the things you did, why you did them and how it impacted on the organization. If you are writing your own resume or you are engaging a professional like me to write it for you, you should keep in mind that today's competitive job market requires more than a presentation of a job description on your resume, LinkedIn profile and during the interview. Employers want to hire a results-driven professional with a proven track record of excellence in their roles. It is up to you or your resume writer to define your accomplishments so that you stand out from the competition.

Here are my recommendations:

When you describe your job show the scope of your role so that employers have a picture of the size and responsibility level of your roles. Theses would include, as applicable, company or department size, budget managed, staff supervised, products created or managed, range – local or global.

Here is an example of what I mean:

- Managed 10 staff and a budget of $250k annually, creating over $3.2M in annual revenues.
- Supported 20 staff in corporate office, including CEO, overseeing over 50 field and offshore locations across the globe.

We don't need 20- bullets to create the context of your role for the employer. Once you set the table, your next objective is to define key accomplishments throughout your career. You want to paint a picture. Why not have the Mona Lisa of resumes? Describe measurable results, quantifiable if you can, or qualifiable at least: decreased costs, increased revenues or sales, reduced time, increased efficiency, eliminated waste, solved emergency situations. identified and solved problems, streamlined operations or systems, expanded customer base, retained customers by promoting customer loyalty, improved reliability, turned around a failing operation (e.g. turn-around specialist), acquired talent that resulting in high performing teams, increased service levels, built new key partnerships

Here are some examples:

- Increased revenue by 700% over three years by developing strategic partnerships with the top ten engineering companies in New York.
- Increased market share by introducing niche technical services to respond to a need of innovative new approaches that drove revenue from $700K annually to $2.5 million.
- Reduced support ticket turnaround from two weeks to three days by developing and launching an automated ticketing and escalation system
- Saved over $750k in the first year by proactively renegotiating all supplier contracts; and improved customer satisfaction by introducing third party quality
-

I also recommend that you create a section in the resume for Awards and Recognition. This is another way to communicate your value. These can be: awards and recognition received, promotions and special assignments, performance evaluation results, company or department awards, and customer satisfaction ratings, to name a few. A few examples of how you can write these:

- Awarded "Customer Service Representative of the Year for three consecutive year, maintaining a 98% customer satisfaction rating
- Created ABC Product, which received the "Product of the Year" Award by XYZ.
- Consistently received 5/5 in annual performance reviews and promoted twice during tenure.

One of the companies that I write for asks clients to complete a simple worksheet to assist their resume writers to provide the client's value proposition to employers. Here is simple worksheet format that they developed for each accomplishment that you can use:

Situation:	As new marketing director found that the company had no jobs in the pipeline, no proposals pending, and had three contracts that were due to terminate in the next year. Company annual revenue was $700,000.
Accomplishment:	Set out to rebrand the company by revamping its marketing materials, develop strategic partnerships in the industry by reintroducing the firm, and demonstrating the value of the company to prospects.
Result:	Positioned the company to gain three important subcontracts that generated $2.1 million within one year, increasing revenue by 300%

HERE IS A WORKSHEET FORMAT YOU CAN USE FOR ASSISTING ME IN SHOWING VALUE TO EMPLOYERS WHEN I RECREATE YOUR RESUME.

JOB TITLE: EMPLOYER:

Situation:	
Accomplishment:	
Result:	

JOB TITLE: EMPLOYER:

Situation:	
Accomplishment:	
Result:	

ADVICE ABOUT APPLICANT TRACKING SYSTEM SOFTWARE THAT COMPANIES USE TO SELECT APPLICANTS FOR INTERVIEWS

By Al Palumbo, MBA, CPRW

Today I want to talk about Applicant Tracking Systems and the misleading ads you may see from resume companies and the promises they make about making your resume pass the Applicant Tracking System software that almost all Fortune 500 companies use to screen out resumes from applicants in response to their job postings.

They promise that the resume that they prepare, when scanned with ATS technology will "ensure passage". I beg to differ. I have been writing resumes professionally for the past six years. I have an exceptionally high placement rate based on feedback, and because I write for a highly respected company that provides transition services to people who are furloughed, I know from the scorecard they give me each week that the majority of folks I am working with land jobs within three months.

Recently a client asked me if there was a way to see if his resume would pass the ATS screening process.   Here was my response:

There is no single test for your resume to determine ATS scoring. That is because each employer has its own criteria for scoring the resume, and the resume is scored against the specific keywords that are within their job postings. In fact, the emphasis by each employer posting the exact same job can vary depending on what they are searching for.

A good resume writer will help you to get the best possible score if the client provides specific job postings that represent the target job they are pursuing. First, it is important that the resume is ATS friendly…no text boxes, tables, headers and footers with important information, graphics, etc. These graphics confuse ATS systems and information contained often cannot be properly scanned with present ATS technology.

Resumes need to have KEYWORDS somewhere in the resume. These are the qualifications or attributes that the job poster reveals in the job posting. For example, say a client wants to apply for a CONSTRUCTION MANAGEMENT position. I will ask the client to provide me with a posting he/she wants to apply for, or as many postings as they are interested in. I will read each of them, extract a composite list of key words, and place them on the resume. I will then ask the client to review my draft and scratch out anything that does not apply to them (they need to be able to defend what I write for them). There is no way for me to know if there are other criteria the employer is using to score a resume, but I am leveling the playing field for my client by addressing what we do know.

In the example of CONSTRUCTION MANAGEMENT, one poster is looking for a candidate that can perform **design review** and **value engineering** in the preconstruction phase of the project. Another poster is not emphasizing this but is looking for someone who is experienced in **building system commissioning**. The client should place as many of these keywords into their resume that applies to them. This will increase your score, but I caution clients…be honest, and don't claim skills you don't have just to get a higher ATS score.

If clients work in partnership with their writers, they will be more successful in a shorter time period. When I furnish the resume, in MS Word, I tell clients that these should be edited for EACH JOB they apply for. If the resume is done correctly, this is a five minute "tweak", mostly of key words. This advice also applies to technology that is specified. I tell clients that if they are familiar with the technology, list it, because sometimes this is a critical aspect of selection.

ARE YOU A DO-ER OR AN ACHIEVER? WHAT DOES YOUR RESUME SAY YOU ARE?

By Al Palumbo, MBA, CPRW

There are four main parts to a modern resume. The first is the Executive Summary that, if constructed correctly, answers the question, "Why should we hire you?" Next is a core skills section that lists keywords that job posters have identified that apply to the applicant. Then comes the work experience section of the resume, followed by a section for education, certifications, and professional development.

The Do-er vs. The Achiever

Many resumes that come across my desk from clients read like a job description. We like to call these the "do-er' resume. It basically reads like a job description but doesn't tell the reader what you achieved during your tenure in the job. The alternative is the "achiever" Resume that demonstrates your value to the employer.

Know Your Value!

The resume is a marketing and branding tool that you are using to entice employers to interview you. Most clients, struggle when I ask them to talk to me about accomplishments. Once I talk them through it and give them some time to contemplate what they have done for their employer, I usually get a nice list of achievements. I find that this is a good exercise:

Number one, they are co-writing this section of the resume with me, and

Number two, they are preparing themselves for the interview. They are able to answer the question, "Why should we hire you?" Once you figure out your accomplishments you have arrived at your Value Proposition.

There are several steps that I coach clients through to find their personal value proposition. If you can answer these questions for each of your current and past jobs, you are on the way to creating a resume that demonstrates your value and lets the reader immediately know that you are a player who will contribute to growth.

Let's start with your current, or most recent job.

Answer these questions:

What was the primary line of business, what was its revenue and did it grow while you were there?

What were the daily functions of the job, and what challenges did you have to overcome to do the job well or improve the way things were being done?

If you were promoted, why did they promote you?

Did the company revenue increase while you were there and by how much or what percentage?

How did you contribute to the increase in revenue?

Did you recommend ways to increase revenue, and if so by how much? Did market share increase and were you a contributor to this?

Did you come up with ways to improve operations that resulted in savings to the company?

What do your performance evaluations say about you?

Wordsmithing

Here are ways that you can describe your accomplishments for each job that you list on your resume:

1. Contributed to.......

2. Partnered and collaborated with....

3. Helped to....

4. Member of task force that....

5. Selected for team that....

6. Directed the team in.....

In conclusion:

- ▸ Make a bulleted list of your accomplishments for each job.
- ▸ Briefly describe the function of the job and then pivot to accomplishments.
- ▸ Remember, accomplishments do not necessarily have to quantifiable.
- ▸ It is just as important to describe how you contributed to profitability, cost savings, training and development of team members, improvement in existing processes, penetration of new accounts, and new markets and any other contributions that helped to grow the organization.

WHEN IT COMES TO RESUMES, DON'T PUT THE CART BEFORE THE HORSE

By Al Palumbo, CPRW, MBA

I have many clients who contact me for a new resume. When I ask them what type of position they are applying for they often say, "I thought I would start with a new resume and then start putting it out there." My response is always the same. I ask them if they just want a pretty resume or a marketing and branding tool that will get results.

Today, resumes are going thorough employer applicant tracking systems and these systems are looking for key words pertinent to the job that is being advertised. The more key words that appear on the resume, the greater the chance of being selected for an interview. So, if you have had the experience of submitting a resume for a job that you knew you were perfect for and didn't get a response, perhaps it is because you were using one resume for all jobs. I am willing to bet that if I reviewed the resume and the job you applied for, I would find that most key words were missing.

My point is simple- Don't get a fancy resume done for $150 - $300 (I write these for clients) without having a focus. Even after you have an appropriate resume for your experience and qualifications, you will always want to focus the resume on the job posting. There will be new key words that are being emphasized, and if they are within your skill set add them to your resume, and you can even take out some that aren't highlighted and save them for later when another posting comes up looking for those key words.

Remember that the average applicant screener or employer spends about six seconds on your resume to decide if it will be read. At the top of the resume is usually a heading, something like "Career Summary" or "Career Profile". Think about putting a heading that matches the job. Immediately you are marketing yourself for the position. Next comes a summary of who you are. Look at the job posting. They often provide a profile about the ideal candidate. If you see yourself in that description, put it in the executive summary at the top of the resume.

Next, I recommend a section that says something like "Highlights" or "Key Skills". What I do here is provide a three-column list of words or very short phrases that come right out of the job posting. Those are the words that an applicant tracking system scans for and they need to be on your resume, there or somewhere else on your resume real estate.

If you are looking for a job or just want to test your value, your resume is a very important marketing tool. One size never fits all. You need to have a good, solid resume that briefly describes your functions but emphasizes accomplishments. Once this is in place, customizing the resume is the best way to have a return on your investment of time (if you write it) or money (if someone writes it for you).

PART I - RESUME DISASTERS

The purpose of a resume is to provide a summary of your skills, abilities, and accomplishments. A resume is not an autobiography and should never be over-encumbered by details. As a certified professional resume writer, I routinely work with clients that are convinced that their resume should document everything they have ever done in their careers. The mistake is that when you do this it is too long, it is extremely boring, and nobody will want to read it, especially if you have submitted it in response to a job posting on line or posted on a company website.

An effective resume is an advertisement of who you are. You are branding yourself by providing a summary of your skills, abilities, and accomplishments. It is a snapshot taken in a point in time in your career. It is your primary tool for the job search, and that is what makes a crisp, clean, accomplishment-driven resume the gold standard of job hunters.

Types of Resumes

There are three basic kinds of resume formats that are generally acceptable to recruiters. The one that recruiters like the best is the **Chronological Format.** This format is preferred by recruiters because they can easily track your employment history and see how long you have worked in a job. For those of you who have a consistent employment history without serious gaps, and who are looking for work in the same or similar field that you are in now, this is your best choice. This format is widely accepted. The work history is in reverse-chronological format, with the last job entered first.

There are circumstances when the chronological resume may not be the best choice. If you have significant gaps in your work history, or are switching careers, this may be the format for you. The **Functional Resume** places emphasis on your skills and accomplishments. Recruiters sometimes do not like this format because it can be hard to pinpoint experience and accomplishment to the work timeline on the resume.

The next option is a combination of the chronological resume and the functional resume, and is known as a hybrid or **Combined Format.** This format allows you to describe your functional skills and related qualifications, and is followed by a reverse chronological employment history. Recruiters and hiring managers like this type of resume format because it allows you to describe qualifications near the top of the resume, and then providing the reverse chronological timeline that employers like to see. When we prepare a combination resume, we provide a career summary at the top of the resume, following by a key skills section of key words, and then the employment history. This format is good for students, new grads, entry level applicants, workers with a steady employment history, career changes (not a radical change), older workers, and applicants re-entering the labor market.

Resume Disasters

Fonts

There are resumes that clients have written that nightmares are made of. Let's start with the font. The type of font you use is the most important design choice you can make. The font, believe it or not, leaves the reader with impressions about your personality, style, and professionalism. Who knew there could be all this fuss about a font?

Here is what you need to keep in mind. The average resume is scanned for six seconds before the reader decides whether to exile the resume to a black hole in cyberspace or continue to read it in more depth. If the resume is well written, without typos, without an offensive sounding email address, and without crazy fonts, pictures, and other things that people do to desecrate the resume, it will get attention.

Regardless of the font you use, it needs to be aesthetically pleasing to the eye. With so many fonts, the choices can be daunting. What you want to accomplish with the font selection is to gain the attention of the reader. Most resumes are either written in a serif font such as Cambria and New Times Roman, or in a san-serif font, such as Calibri and Arial. There are certain fonts that you need to avoid. These include fonts with weird names like Lucinda's Hand, Comic Sans, and Brush Script. Some resume experts like the san-serif fonts, others like serif fonts. In my opinion, it is a matter of taste because both types of fonts are easy to read. Some readers think that the serif fonts project reliability and authority. Other readers like the clean lines and simplicity of non-serif fonts.

Beware of Non-Professional Emails on your Resume

A recent study found that job candidates with quirky, unprofessional email addresses are generally rated lower by potential employers than those with professional names. So loose the email address like this: studmaster44@yahoo.com, and replace it with AlfredHinkle@yahoo..com. Using a simple email with your name is much more professional.

Typos

In a recent survey by of hiring managers from the nation's top 1,000 largest companies by Accounttemps, 40% said one error on the resume is enough for them to stop reading it. One false move on the key board can ruin your chances for that dream job. Many employers believe that if you are sloppy with an important personal document like your resume, this same sloppiness and lack of attention to detail will probably be reflected in your work.

Lack of Focus

Your resume must be focused to the job you are applying for. The standard one size fits all resume may work at McDonald's but it will not work for a mid to senior level professional or executive. The reader should not have to work hard to figure out the job you are applying to. The employer has listed job qualifications and requirements including training and experience. The expectation is that you will only apply if you are qualified, and that means that you have the experience that is specified in the job posting. At the top of the resume, below your name and contact information, there is a headline and a summary that introduces you. If the position is for a project manager, and you have that experience, your headline can say "PROJECT MANAGER". The reader now knows exactly what position you are applying for.

Vagueness

It is maddening if you read someone's resume and still have no idea what they did of accomplished. First, get rid of all the acronyms that nobody outside of your company understands. Unless the acronym is well known in the industry, don't assume that readers of your resume, including screeners, will know what you are talking about. Second, describe the basic functions, but do not provide a laundry list of everything you have ever done. Remember, this is a marketing tool, not a job description, so get to the point. A few bullets under each job describes the heart of what you did, and another few bullets discuss your accomplishments. You do not want 10 or 15 bullets under each job. Five or six would be ideal.

White Space

Your resume needs to be easy to read. If you are worried about putting everything on one page, with tiny margins and tiny fonts, and if the resume is not visually attractive and hard on the eyes, it won't pass the six second test. If you are an experienced professional, your resume does not have to be one page.

THE ART OF THE COVER LETTER

By Al Palumbo, CPRW, MBA

- ➤ *The following is from an article I wrote for an internally based resume writing service that I was a featured resume writer for.*
- ➤ *It tells you everything you need to know about a cover letter and its use in the job search.*
- ➤ *Given the opportunity, you should always provide a cover letter, it gives you the opportunity to highlight, in your own words, your passion for what the organization does and why you should be a part of the team.*
- ➤ *When an employer creates a job posting, they are basically providing you with a checklist of what they are looking for.*
- ➤ *It's OK to mimic the job description, not verbatim but in your own words. The cover letter can then highlight, right off the resume, some key accomplishments or skills that are valuable and relevant to the position.*
- ➤ *Specifics are good -facts, percentages, numbers, and these paint the picture of who you are and why the employer should interview you.*

1. **What does a good cover letter look like?**

Before we answer this question, let's review the purpose of a cover letter. It is important to realize that your cover letter may be the deciding factor in whether you obtain a job interview. This document is a very important component of the job search! The purpose of the cover letter is to tell the prospective employer why you are qualified for the job you are applying for. The cover letter is not a repetition of your resume. It should provide some specifics about why you are a strong candidate. If your resume has been carefully written to provide strong accomplishments, excerpts from the resume with major accomplishments can be placed into the cover letter. Your cover letter is akin to a sales pitch. You are marketing your credentials and you can make the "sale" if you demonstrate your value.

 Here is the basic outline of the cover letter that we recommend:

Header – The cover letter should include your information and the employer's contact information (name, address, phone number, email). If you are applying to a posting on line and do not have the employer's address, you can look up the company and address it to the corporate headquarters.

Salutation – The cover letter salutation begins with "Dr./Mr./Ms. Last Name". If you are not provided with the name of the employer, you can write, "Dear Hiring Manager" or "Dear Hiring Professional". Try not to use "To Whom It May Concern", which is a bit too generic.

Introduction – Start by identifying the job you are applying for. You should note where you heard about the job, such as from a job board, their company website, or a contact associated with the company. Tell the reader, in a few words, how your skills and experience are a great match for the job. What you want to do in this section is get the attention of the reader.

Body – This section is one or two paragraphs that explain why you are interested and why you are the best candidate for the job. In this section, you should mention your relevant qualifications. You should provide specific examples that demonstrate your abilities.

Closing – In this section of your cover letter, summarize how your skills make you a good fit for the job. Tell the reader that you would like an opportunity for an interview. Explain how you will follow-up, and when (if you can), and thank the employer for their consideration of your application.

Signature - Use a complimentary close (Respectfully yours, Sincerely, Very truly yours, etc.) and end the cover letter with your signature (if you are sending a hard copy), followed by your typed name. If it is being downloaded or emailed, just include your typed name.

Your cover letter's layout should be a clean format with enough white space to make it easy to read, and no distracting designs. The cover letter should mirror the layout of a typical business letter, there should be sufficient space between the heading, the salutation, each paragraph, the closing, and your signature. The letter should be written in single space and left-justified.

2. What Font Type Should I Use on My Cover Letter?

You should use a simple font for your cover letter. It is important to use a font that is clear and easy to read. If the cover letter is not instantly legible, it may be discarded, especially if the reader is sorting through many applications.

The most popular fonts to be found on resumes and cover letters are: Arial, Calibri, Verdana, Cambria, and Times New Roman. They are ideal because they are easy to read and present a professional document. The cover letter should avoid underlining and italicizing. Boldfacing can be used to emphasize quantifiable achievements, but should be used sparingly.

3. What are Some Examples of a Good Cover Letter?

The cover letter is a narrative extension of your resume. It should be short and to the point, and be written to prompt the reader to look at the attached resume. A good cover letter will provide the prospective employer with: the reason you are applying, your career paths, your professional history, your skills, and a request for an interview. The cover letter should contain the most important highlights of your resume. The best way to list these are in one or two sentence bullet points. The cover letter should complement and support your resume, but not duplicate it. It is often the first impression that a potential employer will have from you and will prompt a review of the attached resume. Your cover letter should not be a form letter. Form letters are just another form of junk mail! The cover letter needs to tell the reader why you should be interviewed for the position. This is where you make the case for employment by describing your skills, experience, and accomplishments and how this relates to the job you are applying for.

The cover letter can also provide information that doesn't belong in the resume, but could be pertinent to your application. For example, if you are planning to relocate, you can state the facts in the cover letter, and your availability to start work. If you are a career changer, you can indicate that you are looking for the opportunity to apply your skills and abilities to the employer. If you are a recent graduate or completed new technical training, your cover letter can describe your training and certifications, and that you are ready to leverage your skills in your next career move.

There is no resume "silver bullet" in crafting a great cover letter, but there are some best practices to help your application stand above others. A well-written cover letter introduces you, establishes your credentials, and inspires the reader to learn more about you. Here are some best practices that result in impactful cover letters:

Address the letter to a specific person if possible. If you take time to learn who to send the letter to, it is a strategic way of demonstrating your interest in the position. The tone of the cover letter should be semi-formal and business-like, and only contain comments and information that present you as a viable candidate for the position. Personalize the letter with a comment about the organization you are applying to, and use the first-person format. Keep sentences and paragraphs simple and short. If the letter quickly gets to the heart of your reason for applying, it will be appreciated by the reader.

Organizations seek candidates that can provide solutions to the problems and needs. Your letter can demonstrate your sensitivity to problems and ability to deliver solutions. Use a conversational style, not one that is rambling or witty. Some of your personality should come through, but the focus should be on understanding their needs and offering value. The cover letter is not autobiographical, and should focus on how you meet the employer's needs. Minimize the use of the word "I", especially at the beginning of each sentence. The cover letter should explain how you can add value to the job and the role, and the cover letter should be tailored to the specific job you are applying for. The cover letter sells you as a candidate by providing the reasons why you should be invited for an interview. The best cover letters provide specific accomplishments in your career that brought value to the organization, and that are relatable to the job you are applying for

4.   What Should I Include in My Cover Letter?

The cover letter should have specific information including a contact section, a salutation, an introduction, information about why you are qualified for the job, a closing, and your signature. Your goal is to make the case to be selected for an interview. With some research, you can get a name to send the letter to if this is possible. A hiring manager will pay more attention to an application addressed to them personally. The intro gets the attention of the reader. Quickly get across what you can do for them. Use the intro to sell yourself, by citing accomplishments.

Back up the sell in the introduction by providing examples of accomplishments in the body of the letter. This is most effective if written as a list of bullet points that tie talents to the needs of the job. Quickly close the letter by summarizing what you are offering and why your skills will benefit the company, Follow this with a request to follow-up with you at their convenience.

5.   What are Some General Cover Letter Writing Tips?

The cover letter should be brief and to the point. Demonstrate that you meet or exceed the requirements listed in the job description. Convey your interest and your availability to start work. Avoid negatives such as the reason you are leaving or left an employer, or gaps in your employment dates. These negatives are best delivered in person.

Avoid salary history, even if requested. This information can work against you. You can consider providing a range, rather than an exact amount. Make sure the cover letter is easy to read and easy to scan. There should be no text boxes, photographs, tables, or graphics that can confuse applicant tracking systems used to scan applications. Remember that headers and footers can not be read by scanning or applicant tracking systems. Avoid a generic cover letter and the use of clichés.

Explain special skills and qualities that make you uniquely qualified, and do not use clichés such as "I am a self-starter". Use proactive words (e.g., achieved, accomplished, developed, delivered). Tailor the cover letter to the specific organization. Try to demonstrate some knowledge of the employer, often available on the organization's website or on the web.

6.   Do I Need to Make a Different Cover Letter for Each Job I Apply To?

Every cover letter should be tailored to the position that you are applying for. You can use a standard format for each letter, but you should customize each letter that you send it to fit the job posting. Mention how you learned about the job in the first paragraph of your cover letter. We suggest you mention something about the company. You can get this from the mission statement on the company website.

Look at the job posting and list the different criteria that the employer is looking for and list the skills and experience you have. The letter should address how your skills match the job or the criteria listed for selection of a candidate.   Don't forget to include keywords in your cover letter. This may increase your chances of being called in for an interview. The hiring manager can quickly see that you may be qualified from the cover letter.

7.   How Do I Write a Cover Letter for a Position That Doesn't Exist or Hasn't Been Advertised?

The basic cover letter is an "application cover letter". This is used to respond to a job advertisement or solicitation. There are other types of cover letters that are used by job applicants. They are not in response to any job, but is part of an effort to prospect or network.

- The prospecting letter in one that is written to inquire about open positions that you may be qualified to fill. You may or may not know if the company is hiring, of may have heard that they were expanding. This letter lets the prospective employer know why you are interested in the company. The letter should also detail your skills and career goals.
- Networking letters are another type of cover letter. These are letters of introduction, referral letters, or network letters. These letters contain recommendations attesting to your skills and accomplishments, and can be written by others on your behalf.

8.   Who Do I Address My Cover Letter To?

There are ways to find out who the person is within the organization is most likely to be reading your cover letter. You may not find the exact person, but someone close enough, so an educated guess wouldn't hurt. Start with the company website. The key person may be listed as one of the company leaders. You can email or call the corporate office and ask who to direct your cover letter to. You can also search on LinkedIn by typing in the company name and finding LinkedIn members that are with the employer. If you can't the contact person, or don't want to do the research, you can always use "Dear Hiring Manager" or "Dear Hiring Professional".

9.   How Do I Write a Cover Letter Opening Statement?
The most important sentences in your cover letter are the first two. You want to stand out right away and gain the reader's attention by explaining why you should be selected for an interview. Be direct, and let the reader know which position you are applying for. If someone has referred you, mention to the contact. You should try to reference an accomplishment in your work history. Show that you are passionate for the work and your enthusiasm. Use keywords from the job posting by listing skills that match what is in the job posting.

10. What's the Best Way to End a Cover Letter?

A cover letter is a formal business letter, so the closing should not be overly casual or friendly. Don't use closings such as: Affectionately, Best wishes, Warm Regards, and no emoticons! If you are sending an email, contact information can be placed below your name, including phone number, email address, and LinkedIn profile URL.

Competitive job seekers often employ strong closes to obtain the interview. Here is an example of a competitive closing: "I look forward to speaking to you personally to discuss your needs and how I can help you to meet them. I will email you within the week to see when your calendar is open". The no-action close ending gives control of the interviewing process to the reader. It indicates that you will wait for a call, and it is not action focused. Here is an example:

 "A copy of my resume is attached for your review and consideration. If my background and experience interests you, I would be pleased to hear from you to discuss how I can contribute to the growth of the company".

Whatever your choice of close, your cover letter should restate your enthusiasm, confirm your desire for the interview, and state what the next step will be. It may be preferable to sue an action close by telling the recipient that you will follow up and when. Sometimes you cannot do this, and will have to wait to be contacted.

11. How Long is a Good Cover Letter?

A good cover letter is never more than one page. It should consist of several paragraphs including bullets to make it easy to read. It should highlight your relevant qualifications and what you are offering. Most employers prefer a cover letter that is less that a full page.

12. Can I Write a Cover Letter in First Person?

The cover letter should always be written in the first person. The cover letter is the first opportunity to provide a good impression and start a rapport with the reader. The application is from you and is all about you, so first person is the most appropriate format.

13. Do I Need to Sign a Cover Letter I'm Going to Send Digitally?

It's not necessary to add a physical signature to an electronic document like a cover letter. It is not a binding agreement of any kind. Simply close by typing your name.

14. Should I Mention My Past Salary in a Cover Letter?

It is not a good idea to mention salary in the cover letter if it is not requested. It can either screen you out automatically or sell yourself short in a negotiation. Sometimes there is a specific request for salary history. The best way to respond to this is to provide an acceptable salary range, such as "$60,000 to $65,000, not including benefits". You can also state that requirements are flexible and negotiable, and can be discussed at the interview.

NOTES:

NOTES:

www.ingramcontent.com/pod-product-compliance
Lightning Source LLC
Chambersburg PA
CBHW081515220526
45467CB00010B/2927